Dear Ella;

Hope and faith r the key to all that we shall ever be!!

Love,
Ella D. A. Russ

Healing the Hurt

by
Delores Russ

authorHOUSE™

1663 LIBERTY DRIVE, SUITE 200
BLOOMINGTON, INDIANA 47403
(800) 839-8640
WWW.AUTHORHOUSE.COM

First published by AuthorHouse 07/01/05

ISBN: 1-4208-5091-1 (sc)

Library of Congress Control Number: 2005903784

Printed in the United States of America
Bloomington, Indiana

This book is printed on acid-free paper.

ACKNOWLEDGMENTS

I want to thank and give my appreciation to the following persons who have blessed and enriched my life in so many ways. The former members of the Christian Women and Men in Ministry Fellowship, Inc.; Bishop Erwin Scofield, what a precious servant; Pastor Dena S. Jobes and Elder Albert S. Jobes, my friends and current Pastors; my daughters, Shirley and Peggy; my grandson Kendrick; Pastor Jacqueline McCullough; Bishop and Mother Monroe R. Saunders, Sr., my spiritual parents; Dr. Lois McMillan, English Professor of Morgan State University and Minister Lillian Watters, who has a mighty testimony of God's tremendous, mighty, healing power from past injuries and pain.

Contents

INTRODUCTION

I was inspired by the Holy Spirit to pen this book after talking with and ministering to so many precious, gifted sisters in Christ who love God and who are striving with all their heart to please Him and to move forward in their God–given potential and destiny, but find the reach very difficult because of the devastating pains and hurts of their past.

As I travel to various states ministering at different retreats, women's conferences and workshops, I encounter so many, many hurting sisters. Upon entering the meeting room, I begin to sense that there is an expectation in the air from those women, especially those who have come hoping that this is their time to be set free. As I enter the room, settle down in my seat and begin to look out into the audience, the Holy Spirit allows the gift of discernment to be activated. No matter how well one speaks or dresses, the Holy Ghost becomes a detector and discerner of every need, hurt, and pain in one's life, even the intent of the heart. The Spirit searches all things, yea, even the deep things!

Somewhere in the course of my message, teaching or self disclosure (which are many) the Holy Spirit hits the target and boomerangs in on the pains and hurts in the spirit of this or that sister, causing some to express their inward emotions then and there. Some scream, some holler, falling to the floor on their hands and knees crying uncontrollably. Of course, I am always compelled by the Holy Spirit to stop and to do direct ministering at that moment, with someone assisting me in doing so.

Then there are those who sit quietly with tears streaming down their faces, and then there are those who will come and ask for my home telephone number or ask at what hotel I am staying. This group is like Nicodemus who came to Jesus by night because they do not want others to know that they do not have it all together. In the confines of my hotel room, at home or on my telephone, long hours, many days and months afterward are spent talking and walking through the debris of their broken lives because they desire to be free. I am never offended or bothered by these contacts because I am the handmaiden of God, and I remembered how I wished that I would have had someone to walk with me through my brokenness!

How I can identify with my sisters is because of the many, many past pains, hurts and agonies that I experienced in my own life. Today, I am free because of the wonderful, marvelous, stupendous dealings of God's mercies and power in my life. It was this power and mercy that removed those crippling elements from me, and brought clarity and freedom to my life. People, say, "God is good all the time," but I say, "God is good on overtime" because I was worthy of death, but He gave me another chance to make my life right. In fact, as I look back, I realize that God gave me so many, many, many chances until I could come to myself and put on strength to fight back,(my testimony is shared later in the book); Therefore, I am working on overtime. – **How Longsuffering Is Our God!!!**

I thank God for the former Christian Women and Men In Ministry Fellowship, Inc., which was an Interdenominational ministry, whose utmost endeavor and concern was that other women and men would find freedom, peace, deliverance, and be empowered by the Holy Ghost for which Christ died. For 15 years, the Lord allowed me along with the precious ministers and members of this ministry to encounter and minister to hundreds of women (and men) who had walked through the dry places of life, and who had never experienced healing from the past because they had never been exposed to an atmosphere where love was paramount or where the Spirit of God was allowed to have free course without hindrance.

The Lord allowed the CWIMF, Inc., as well as other ministers and ministries to create an atmosphere which is not programmed or oriented by "man–made" rules and doctrines, where these hurting women and men can come without pretense and "let it all go", or "let it all hang out." We were willing to labor all night, if need be, in order to assist in the process of the Holy Spirit's intervention; O, how we need more spiritual midwives and orderlies who are not afraid to get dirty, and who will roll up their sleeves and labor with souls until they are delivered. Yes, we need those who are willing to be workmen together with Christ.

My prayer and motto is, "Lord do what you do best, and that is freeing people from the inside out." The Lord is a specialist in getting rid of dead men's bones and cleaning the inside of the cup so that pure light can shine from the inner person to the outward person.

Therefore, this book is dedicated to those sisters whose childhood dreams and security were shattered by one means or another. I pray that the writing on these pages will inspire you to know that there is help, hope, health and healing. This book is not intended to cry a sad story or to place blame. It is not a book of statistical data, nor is it a book full of pretty words and pretty pictures, but it is a book that looks at the reality in lives of so many women who need to know that they can be free from pain; they can be free from the "sea of the past" that has caused them to almost drown, going down for the last time and not wanting to come up, only to die!

God's Handmaiden
Delores A. Russ

PREFACE

Jesus said in John 10:10 (KJV): "I come that they might have life, and that they might have it more abundantly." The same chapter and verse in the Living Bible states: "The thief's purpose is to steal, kill, and destroy. My purpose is to give life in all its fullness."

Since this abundant life is to be experienced in all its fullness (love, joy, and peace in the Holy Ghost) by every believer, then something is wrong, lacking or missing when those who are members of the body of Christ are continuously attacked, harassed and plagued by the thief, satan and are unable to repel his attacks because of a very weak, run—down immune system which is brought about by constant untreated pain, hurt, and anger from the past.

But worst of all, the strong members of the body of Christ who themselves have been delivered and strengthened, leave those weak members unattended and unassisted in apprehending and appropriating the abundant life, allowing satan to wreak havoc with these persons' spiritual well being. While satan is ravishing and sapping the little life and strength out of the feeble members, we stand by in self—contentment, self—righteousness, judgement and condemnation. The question arises: Is God pleased with our actions?

There is a desperate need that the wounded and broken members of Christ's body experience the complete healing and fullness of Christ within their inner being. Oh, Yes, for some, the outward person appears to have it all together, but the Spirit of God does discern all things; yea even the deep things. There is nothing hid from the eyes of God, nor from those whom He have given the gift of discernment to look beyond the surface things.

The gift of discernment is not given to be nosy, to meddle, or for curiosity sake, but it is given to move in the realm of the Spirit to make a difference, to bring about a change and take the action the way Jesus would have done. What action did Jesus take? He went where the sick, downcast, the lepers, the sinners, the dead, and the hungry were and met them where they were. He brought healing and restoration to their situation! Well, now, has not God given and committed unto us this same Ministry of Reconciliation (2 Cor. 5:18–21)? The church has been commissioned to stand in Christ's stead in the earth today, as sons of God, to utilize and demonstrate the same power that Jesus had with the Father while He was on the earth. The question arises: Are We Using It???

I am afraid that many have this gift of discernment and the authority to reconcile people unto God, but they are not coming alongside the weak, uncomely members, using this gift to bring wholeness to the entire body of Christ through love, mercy, longsuffering, and compassion:

> "Nay, much more of those members of the body, which seem to be more feeble, are necessary: And those members of the body which we think to be less

honorable, upon these we bestow more abundant honor, and our uncomely parts have more abundant comeliness. For our comely parts have no need: but God hath tempered the body together, having given more abundant honor to that part which lack. ICor. 12:22–24 (KJV)

In other words, our spiritual sisters and brothers have been "kicked to the curb" in their brokenness and weakness because we see them as always crying the blues, having a pity–party, and we are sick of fooling with them. We see them as a hopeless, "Basket Case." **But God reminds us that they are still a part of you and His body, whether we like it or not. We are responsible to God for how we treat them: "Whether one member suffers; all members suffer with it; or one member be honored, all rejoices with it." (I Co. 12:28)**

We, the church of Jesus Christ and those of the five fold ministries must, or should I say better, get our act together. We must stop trying to be so great and wonderful in our own names and become united under the banner and Name of Jesus Christ, who paid that awful price for souls: For there is no other name given under the heavens whereby men can be saved except the Name of Jesus, not our name!

We must stop shunning our duty and arise to the occasion for which we have been called and that is: "For the perfecting of the saints, for the work of the ministry, for the edifying of the body of Christ: till we all come into the unity of the faith, and of the knowledge of the Son of God, unto a perfect man (no gender), unto the measure of the stature of the fullness of Christ" (Eph. 4:12,13 – KJV). God is holding us accountable! The blood of souls is on our hands!!!

We must not let another "wounded soldier die!!! I repeat, WE Must Not Allow Another One of God's Wounded Soldiers Lie on the Battlefield of Life and Die!!! When one member of the body of Christ is left to die or left unattended to bleed to death, God is holding us accountable; What will we answer God? We must stop operating on the worthy and unworthy principle: who is fit or unfit to receive the blessings, mercies, and the healing of God, or who is fit to inherit eternal life and who is fit to receive God's forgiveness – only God has that authority of decision. I wonder what we would do today with the woman in the scripture who was caught in adultery, since we cannot even deal with those people (saints) who do not come to church every time the church door is opened, or those people who do not look and act according to our status–quo?

Jesus told Simon Peter: "Satan has asked to have all of you, to sift you like wheat." But, I have pleaded in prayer for you, Simon, that your faith should not fail. So when you have repented and turned to me again, <u>strengthen and build up your brother</u>" (Lu. 22:31–31 – LB).

I pray that we will encourage the strong members to keep on being strong. I also pray that we will continue to win souls into the kingdom of God, but I pray above all that "As we have therefore opportunity, <u>let us do good unto all men, especially unto them who are of the household of faith</u>." (Eph. 6:10). The good that we can do unto the household of faith is to extend tenderness, compassion, love, mercy, long–suffering, and understanding to every member, and shame on us if we don't since none of us are not far removed from the suffering of others (see Gal. 6:1–2).

Those members who we just can't be bothered with – the unlovely – will become the greatest asset the church has. After their deliverance, they will be a living testimony and witness of God's profound love and healing power to those who would be saved and to the many weak souls who feel that there is no way out. They will become mighty weapons against the kingdom of darkness.

Those of us who are indeed true and loving parents would not throw the baby out with the bath water, nor would we ignore or treat one child differently from the other, even though one may be different. But we take time to develop each child because we love them, and they are bone of our bone and flesh of our flesh. Yes, we may sometimes become impatient, but we continue to remember that the seed was imparted to daddy by God, and the mother carried that child in her body for nine months; therefore, we seek to bring out the best in each child; so must the spiritual children of God be cared for even though one may be different from the other. This care must not only be given by God, but also by the church, the body of Christ, which has been left in the earth in Christ's stead.

Remember, all souls belong to God, and He is not in the casting away or condemning business, but in reaping the harvest. His timing is not our time, nor His mind our mind. As we acquire the mind and attitude of God, we will be willing and in submission to the timing of God to make all souls and all things new!

THE DREAM

For every little girl there is a dream, a dream of growing–up, being happy, and living happily ever after. This happiness includes having good, loving parents who will live forever, a husband, children, and a nice home where peace, love, safety, and comfort dwell.

Even in her pigtails and bobby socks, playing with her dolls and tea–set, she dreams of being protected by her daddy or big brother, being loved by her mother and other siblings, becoming a nurse, a doctor, etc.; Then there is this handsome knight in shining armor who will rescue her from anyone or anything. He will protect her, love her, and fulfill her womanliness which is peeking out her eyes even in childhood. The dream is in her consciousness and subconsciousness. She takes it with her wherever she goes. She is a little girl, yet with big dreams.

Dreams are one of a person's greatest possessions. For in those dreams are one's well–being, one's hope, one's peace, one's joy, one's focus, one's goal; In fact, the "who I am or who I desire to be or become" is encompassed in the dream.

Oh, how startling it is to awake and realize that ones dream has been shattered; — it was only a dream!!! For many, these dreams were shattered very early in life by:

- Abusive parents (physical, verbally, mentally)
- Incest
- Rape
- Lack of Life's necessities (love, food, clothing, shelter)
- Mental Limitations
- Very low self—esteem
- Rejection
- Friends
- Churches (spiritual abuse)
- Broken marriage of parents and remarriage (stepchild)
- Absence of one parent or both
- Foster Home situations

All of this equaled fear, hurt, disappointment, distrust, pain, and confusion. Life became a jungle, and the focus of ones dreams became less and less clear. Through those most difficult, blinding experiences, there was no one there in the process of growth to help us not lose who we were or whom we could become.

We were usually compared with someone else, or we compared ourselves to others, or we were nonexistent. We were called dumb, stupid or other names by those we thought loved us. The more we looked at others whom we felt were so wonderful, the less we felt about our own person. The self—esteem became lower and lower, and we sank deeper and deeper into whom we felt we were not. We were always looking in someone else's "looking glass" and their reflection, never seeing our own selves, never seeing who we were or what we could become in spite of the dark circumstances.

Though the focus of our dreams became less and less clear, and the winds and storms blew against our minds and souls, somehow we held onto our dreams.

Fragmented, yes, distorted, yes, but it was still our dream. Yes, wounded inside and outside, but we held on in spite of it all.

As time passed, this girl entered into adulthood still holding on to the dreams. Eventually, she felt that she had walked into her dream when she met this wonderful, handsome man, who was talking just the right talk, and walking just the right walk. He caused her heart to throb and palpitate. She knew that her knight in shining armor had arrived. Oh boy! When he asked her to marry him, she knew that her dream had been fulfilled. She was in the 7th heaven, only later to find out that the childhood dream was still only a dream, not a reality.

One of the most important relationships that a woman enters into is the intimacy with a male (here I am not talking about sex, but a warm, caring relationship). This is a "biggie," the real deal, the serious "I've arrived stuff"; the courtship and then the marriage. She feels that this is critical to her survival, "Surely I will be all right now," only to discover that the past was still there. The hurt and pain become even greater because she fails to realize that marriage could not compensate for the past issues of her life which had never been resolved. She failed to realize that marriage carried a double responsibility which impacts upon a woman who steps into the role of a wife and mother, especially when she had brought over so

Delores Russ

much excess baggage. Therefore, problems only compound with the unresolved issues.

The reality of the matter was that there were two different persons, with two different backgrounds, expectations, goal, and purposes trying to fuse together. Neither knew how to really give to one another because they both needed to receive so much themselves. Each had separate dreams which were worlds apart; therefore, he could not fulfill hers nor she his.

Suddenly, the newness of marriage wore off; if there ever was a newness, you discovered that this person you married <u>was not an indestructible knight in shining armor, but a human being with</u>:

1. Flesh and bones
2. Bad hygiene (and keep it)
3. Unrealistic expectations and demands of you,
   while he himself had none of his own.
4. No communication skills
5 No affections
6. No time or interest in you
7. Financial problems and poor money management
8. Sexual difficulties and differences
9. Laziness (you became his maid or just an object)
10. Abusive – physical, mentally, and verbally
<u>You stand back and say, "Who or what is this I married"</u>!!

The marriage began to deteriorate slowly but surely. All communication ceased except what was necessary to say, if anything. However, you still tried to hold on to your dream which became: "I can change him if I try harder to love him, if I stroke his ego more, if I try more sexual explorations to excite him more (you even went out and bought a book to teach you all the "know–hows"), or if I am more faithful in my wifely duties then he will surely love me."

Well, did it work? No!, you tried over and over again, still trying to keep your dreams afloat until you finally realized that your effort to change him or the situation was futile and a terrible failure. Not only were you affected and on the verge of a nervous breakdown, but the children, if there were any, were vastly affected. Your world was falling apart, crumbling before your eyes.

Before you knew it, the husband was involved in an affair with another woman whom he said understood him (of course you didn't). Sometimes the partners become involved in bi–sexual relationships (sad to say), and sometimes abuse and incestuous acts are committed in the martial relationship. Interestingly enough, and sad to say that many of these couples claim salvation, go to church regularly, are highly respected and look good, but are living a life of pretense - Oh, there is another story, the real story! However, you forgave over and over again and again trying to still make your dream a reality.

Finally, you cannot take it any more, you are devastated, extremely hurt, worn, torn, and angry. You are not only angry with the husband, but also with God. The marriage ends in separation or divorce, leaving a trail of terrible bitterness, anger, hatred, hurt, extremely damaged emotions, feelings of defeat, and being purely tired of life. Many times, suicide was even contemplated. If there are children who must be reared, the woman is usually left with this tremendous task and responsibility, while so many fathers have a "don't care attitude" (certainly not all), and contribute no financial support nor moral support. Too often, the child out of bitterness and anger is used as a weapon to get even with the mate. We also often overcompensate the child(ren) trying to make up for the missing parent because we are most often too numb to balance our thinking.

The woman is usually blamed for the failure of her marriage, but even more terrible, she blames herself or passes the blame on to something or some one else. She then lives in a world of guilt, beating herself up. She withdraws from meaningful associations or relationships, doing only what is necessary or going only to those places which are necessary. The anger is seething inside of her. She is often on edge, easily annoyed, tense, irritable, indifferent, silent or very apprehensive. Her world has turned upside down, topsy—turvy; it is spinning out of control into a world of pit—blackness. All seems to be lost!!

Deep down inside there are many questions: "Where do I go from here? Is there hope? Can any part of my dream be fulfilled? I thirst for the infusion of new life into my being. The vastness of all that God created is within me, the preciousness of life. In fact, I am impregnated with it; I want it so badly, but I do not know how to deliver it by myself. I need Help, I am desperate, I need to be healed!!!"

No matter what, life must go on no matter the brokenness or fragmentation. The broken and fragmented pieces of your heart can be and must be put back together again to bring wholeness.

THE JOURNEY OF PAIN

Inner pain and healing is as ancient as man. I believe that the heart of God was broken, and He suffered inner pain from the time that His first created beings, Adam and Eve, sinned and disobeyed His commandment not to eat of the tree of the knowledge of good and evil. God made Adam and Eve in His own image and likeness, and breathed into them His own breath. God intended that they should enjoy a holy state of living, with peace and serenity in the perfect dwelling place which He had prepared for them, and there He could commune with His friend, Adam, daily. O' how God's heart must have hurt when He expelled Adam and Eve from the Garden of Eden!! All communion ceased with His friend, Adam.

Jesus appeased and satisfied the heart of God when He became the perfect sacrificial Lamb. It pleased the Father to bruise Jesus in order to give men a way out of sin (Is. 53:5.12). The scripture tells us that Jesus felt forsaken by His Father on the cross, but I also believe that the pain, suffering and agony which He felt on the cross were not just physical pain, but heart pain. No, He did not need inner healing as we do because He was the healer. It was not His pain that

He endured, but our pains and transgressions. The cup was very, very bitter, but He was willing to take the cup for our healing, both soul, spirit, and body.

Even now, I believe that the heart of God is breaking and hurting (inner pain) when men, women, boys, and girls reject the Love of Jesus. Sins open the door allowing different infirmities to come in, whether physical, mental, emotional or spiritual which can and will hold us in bondage. Jesus became the propitiation for our sins and gave us a way out of our dilemma, no matter what it is. God understands our pains, hurts, brokenness and disappointments because He took unto Himself a human body like ours (Jn. 1:14; Phil. 2:7, 8), and suffered much more than we ever will! He became our High Priest and Intercessor, and He now stands with His arms wide open bidding you and me to come — He Is The Healer!!!

Today, we wonder why there is so much emphasis on inner healing from past pain and hurts, and why so many books are being written on the subject: Is it because this is a day of enlightenment, when the Holy Spirit is saying that we do not have to continue to walk around in upheaval and darkness unhealed? Is it because those of us who have walked the long journey of pain and have been released and freed from the prison of pain, hurt, fear, disappointments, anger, people's opinions and brokenness are we reaching out to those who have yet to realize that they too can be free in mind, soul, and spirit by the power of the Holy Ghost? I say, yes, to both of these questions.

Some have accused us of using psychological approaches when we encourage people to look at their past and deal with those unresolved issues that are bottled up within them waiting to explode. I say, no; this is not a fact. We are not using psychology, but we are using the Weapons of the Spirit by assisting the person to tear down those <u>strongholds</u> (a fortified place) which satan has built and has taken residence, and he is having a "field day" holding women and men in captivity (2 Co. 10:3–6; 2 Ti. 2:24–26).

Pulling down those strongholds <u>is the demolition and removal</u> of the old ways of thinking, the pains, hurts, unforgiveness, agony, disappointments, frustrations, rejections, low self–esteem, etc., so that the actual presence of Jesus Christ can be manifested in and through us. Wherein, Christ can be formed in us – His very image – making us new creatures. If we fail to see our relationship to God in any other way, we will allow too many areas within us to remain unchanged. Remember, this is an "inside job."

God's desire is to have His purpose of Holiness fill our very being, thought, and intent which will cause us to become witnesses of His grace, mercy, and love – The Good News of the Gospel. However, these hurting persons will never be messengers of the Good News, whether spoken or visual, nor carry the seed of light when there are yet so many unresolved issues and emotions, and yet so much darkness roaming around in their heads and hearts.

The Holy Spirit did not come just to make us feel good, nor just to put bandages on those wounds and deep cut places, but He came to dig up, root up, cleanse, remove, and get rid of anything and everything that will hinder our spiritual growth. His desire is to restore us to a right and peaceful relationship with Himself and ourselves. The Holy Spirit is not only our comforter, but also our truth. He will lead and guide us into all truth no matter how painful that truth is, or what darkness that truth addresses. The darkness must be dealt with before light can shine through... THE TRUTH WILL SET YOU FREE!!!

Sometimes we wonder why a person acts in such a peculiar manner or why he or she is not easily entreated. Most often, it is because of the devastating life experienced. I have ministered to both male and female who have been victims of incest, rape, abuse (both physical and mental), and other diabolical acts committed over and over again by family members, church members and others whom they trusted. I have found that most of the deep pains that women experience extend back to their childhood, those fragile, developing years (as mine did), or in their "love life" as adults.

These women were traumatized and victimized repeatedly by someone whom they trusted and loved, someone who was responsible for their care and well–being, someone who should have protected them. Those persons were parents, siblings, an aunt, an uncle, a cousin, a teacher, an older playmate, a close neighbor, a husband, or a church member. On most occasions, the traumatizing and victimizing were not addressed, just kept hush–hush or swept under the rug, and the victim was forbidden to talk about what and who! These unresolved issues carried from childhood into adulthood.

These women who were victimized at childhood enter into adulthood and acquire various relationships hoping to find happiness and healing, but they are unable to bond because they really do not know how to trust anyone. This brings about more hurt and pain because they really want to bond, but cannot. Many reach the age of 30, 40, 50, and 70 years old before the issues are resolved and bonding begins (mine was at the age of 40 years old). It's so sad to say that some of these women live all their lives and die still imprisoned, never able to forgive or forget, never living.

These sisters have cried and are still crying for someone to understand them, to look at them without being judgmental or accusing them of having a "pity party", losing their mind, or hearing, as they told me: "You've been saved long enough to have gotten yourself together." These women only want someone who care enough to assist them in getting out of this pit call hurt, loneliness, and depression- they are wounded. They do not want to be totally dependent, but they just need a helping hand to pull up by, and lend nurturing for a season, just as the man who went down from Jerusalem to Jericho and fell among thieves, who stripped him of his raiment, wounded him, leaving him half dead. Along came a priest, and when he saw him he passed by on the other side; along came a Levite, and when he came to the place, he came and looked at him and passed by on the other side. Both the priest and the Levite saw the man naked, severely wounded, bleeding with his skin wide open with infected cuts and bruises, but passed by on the other side without helping to restore the man, or even calling for help.

Thank God for the Samaritan, the non–religious man, who when he saw the man was moved with compassion. He bound him up, poured in oil and wine, set him on his beast and brought him to the inn and gave him personal care himself. Even when the Samaritan had to depart, he left sufficient means to care for the man until his return (Lu. 8:30–36)... What a neighbor!!! The man who fell among thieves did not need attending to all his life, but only until he could recover and gain strength... SO DO THESE SISTERS!

I have sat across the table from my sisters, or next to them, holding their hands, or holding them in my lap, or I have been down on the floor with them as they wept, cried, and screamed violently,

11

hitting the floor in anger. Many were balled up in a fetal position, regurgitating over and over. Some of these women have gone into a state of unconsciousness and the spirit of death came upon them, but by the power and authority of the Holy Ghost, that thief, that killer, that liar, that diabolical evil corrupt one, satan, was commanded to back off and leave in the POWERFUL NAME of JESUS CHRIST – PRAISE GOD!

They have so many, many layers and layers of pains and hurts piled on top of one another. How my heart breaks over and over as I witness their pain, since it take me back to my own. It is so difficult for these sisters to even articulate their feelings because they experience such severe pain and anguish, actually reliving the painful moments as they try to tell their stories and express their feelings. It is sad that others try to tell these sisters' stories who do not know them, and don't even know the stories nor the truth. This is why so many sisters are silent sufferers.

My sisters often feel that they will be condemned or that no one will understand what has happened in their lives and what brought them to where they are. Yes, most of these sisters do go to church, are saved and are faithful members. However, they cannot open up for the fear of "hearing their stories spread all over the church", or "preached on" from the pulpit after they confide in the leader. Therefore, they feel ashamed or feel that they do not fit. They feel that they are walking this road alone, directly facing the storm that won't let up – Their journey has been long, tedious and dangerous. These ladies have given all that they can, but it never seems to be enough.

Most of these sisters have been in search for someone to verify or validate the "Who Am I"; therefore, they go looking for love, but it is often in the wrong places and from the wrong persons. Too often, they accept the first thing that comes along which they feel will make them secure. They find themselves in a whirlwind of love affairs. Many have been threatened with bodily harm or exposure if they end the affair, especially if the affair involves a person of authority who is in a key position, and who has clout with the public. So they are afraid to walk away from the relationship, and find themselves laden with double guilt, deeper despondency and depression... another layer of pain.

Life is so full of life only waiting to be discovered, if we can only move beyond our yesterdays. The today and the tomorrow can be so bright and meaningful if we would only allow ourselves to see through the eyes of God who created us. We are fearfully and wonderfully made and God wants only the best for His sons and daughters. We must allow God to be our today and our tomorrow. I would even dare to say that even our yesterday, for whether we believe it or not, "All things do work together for good, to them who love the Lord, and them who are called according to His purpose." (Rm. 8:28).

In spite of what it looks like or what has happened, He was our yesterday because if He had not been our yesterday, we would not be here today, and there would be no now, nor would there be a tomorrow... yesterday brings us into today and the future if we can but learn from yesterday!! God has always had a purpose and destiny for each of us even before we were born because we were chosen in Him before the foundation of the world.

In our journey from pain toward wholeness, there is no more time to waste, finger pointing or blaming others, nor is there time to accept condemnation from others. There is no time to blame yourself or walk around in guilt rehearsing: If I had not been so stupid, if I had done more, if I had not done this or that, if it had not been for such and such a one, if I had waited; why, why, why; if, if or maybe – questions and more questions. Yes, many times we could have used better judgments or made better choices, but it is done now, and we can't take it back. The only recourse that we now have is to come face to face with the issues and come face to face with God. With all your heart, mind, and soul, seek His divine healing power. Allow Him to answer the questions of the past and bring resolution to the past, and lead you into your new life.

Enough precious moments, energy, and strength have been wasted. It is time to move toward your healing and your Healer, the Lord Jesus Christ. He can bring love and peace in the place of the hurts and turmoil of the past. To verify His intent and purpose in the world and what He could accomplish in us, Jesus said in Luke 3:18–19 (NKJV):

> "The Spirit of the Lord is upon Me, Because He has anointed Me to preach the gospel to the poor; He has sent Me to **heal the brokenhearted, To proclaim liberty to the captive, And recovery of the sight to the blind. To set at liberty those who are oppressed**; To proclaim the acceptable year of the Lord."

It will amaze you what God can and will do for you in the rich abundance of His love, compassion, and mercy:

> "That He may grant you, according to the riches of His glory, to be strengthened with might through

His Spirit in the inner man, that Christ may dwell
in your hearts through faith; that you, being rooted
and grounded in love, may be able to comprehend
with all the saints what is the width, and length, and
depth and height, and to know the love of Christ,
which passes knowledge; that you may be filled with
the fullness of God. ***Now unto Him who is able to
do exceedingly abundantly above all that we can ask
or think, according to the power that works in us.***
Ephesians 3:16–20 (NKJV)

Our spirit must be free as a bird who soars through the air bound
for higher places; So must we be air—borne for higher places in the
Holy Spirit, but we cannot do this with the past tied to our back.
Therefore, we must acknowledge what is weighing us down from the
past or present. We must look it square in the face and deal with
it even as Jacob did when he had to face his brother Esau, whose
birthright he had stolen by deceit. These two brothers had to deal
with past issues between them. Yes, Jacob was afraid of Esau, but
he wanted healing in this matter; therefore, he had no choice but to
come face to face with the one whom he feared and the one he knew
hated him.

After their encounter, Jacob wrestled with a man all night until the
breaking of day, saying, I will not let you go except you bless me. Well,
Jacob's name was changed and he had a limp in his hip, but he came
forth as a new person, with double strength and new determination.
The one most interesting thing about Jacob's encounter with the man
he wrestled with all night was that Jacob said: "for I have seen God

face to face, and my life is preserved" (Genesis 32), so he named the place Peniel. What first appeared to be just a man to Jacob in the night season is now clear to him at the breaking of the day. It was God himself whom Jacob saw!

When your day breaks, you will see God high and lifted up, His train filling the temple, standing with out—stretched arms bidding you to come up higher. You must head for higher grounds where the waters cannot drown you. The Journey has been long, but safety is ahead!!!

WHO CAN CONDEMN

Believe me when I tell you that inner healing from past pains and hurts transcends denominational ties, race, family names, how much money one has, or what city, state, or country one resides in. <u>IT IS REAL</u>!

Perhaps those who have never experienced any great trauma in their lives or to their person cannot identify, but for those of us who know, it is real. I am convinced that if someone falls and merely pricks their finger with only a minor injury, and another person is involved in a severe automobile accident with crushed ribs, broken legs, and severe head injuries, it would require more long–term, **intensive, treatments and care** for the severely injured than for the person who merely pricked his or her finger. No matter who was at fault in the car accident, time is not wasted blaming. Emergency help is called and hospitalization is required, and most likely surgery will be required. If the person survives, the recovery period will be a long process, more for some than others. Many long hours, days, and months will be spent in treatment and recovery.

So is it with those who have suffered great injury to their person. Those who are apart of the intensive care unit cannot afford to stand around finger pointing or blaming the person who caused the accident, nor the person injured, but we must be a part of the emergency rescue squad, nursing team, intensive care unit, and rehabilitation unit.

Beverly LaHaye makes a statement in her book I Am A Woman By God's Design: "It is indeed unfortunate that the widowed Christian woman who has experienced a good marriage is today known as single. This puts her in the same category as a lesbian who has chosen a lifestyle of promiscuity and immorality"(pg 119).

The statement is indeed quite unfortunate because it blames, accuses, and labels. Above all, it is not scripture based. Even if a previously married woman decides to be known as single, this does not mean that she lives a lifestyle of immorality, a state or quality of being immoral, vice, wickedness; unchastity; also an immoral act or practice; Nor does this woman lead a lifestyle of promiscuity: consisting of a heterogeneous (differing in kind, having unlike qualities, dissimilar, opposed to homogenous); a mixture of persons or things; indiscriminately distributed, applied, granted, etc., as promiscuous blame, intercourse; undiscriminating irregular, casual or the like; promiscuous sexual union.

Singleness does not mean that one is lawless, lewd, unrestrained or unchaste; Neither should it be assumed that these women, whether they have never married, separated, divorced or widowed are "swingers." They are not living a loose life, nor are they sexually uncontrolled or uncontrolled in their behavior, and it certainly does not put them in the category of a lesbian in any sense of the word!!!

The truth is that single persons are just as particular as anyone else, or even more so. This is why so many have remained without companions because they will not settle for anyone or anything, nor are they "bed–hoppers", nor are they having inordinate sexual encounters!! They are very discreet and disciplined with godly values. They know that their body is the temple of God; therefore, they have made a choice to have their sexual appetite controlled and kept by and through The Power of the Holy Spirit!!

There are many women whose spouse has died, and they look back and realize that they did have a wonderful mate who should not have died. Then there is the woman whose husband was not so wonderful, but she loved him and stayed in the marriage for one reason or another, even though there was much suffering. This woman, too, also feels that God should not have let her husband die.

Both of these women react by saying something like this: "I will never marry again because no one will ever take my husband's place"; or, "yes, I loved my husband, but I went through too much and never want to marry again." Often, neither one of these women can bring closure to what was, whether good or bad in order to move on; —— they are stuck. Therefore, they chose to live a single life, not single to say I am available for whosoever and whatsoever. They do not try to hide the fact that they were previously married, nor should their femininity be in question.

We do not need to be labeled, whether we had a good or a bad marriage, whether widowed, divorced, separated or never married. We have enough to encounter as it is without being labeled, especially by someone who has not walked where we have walked.

There is a great fight of affliction being directed at God's people from the kingdom of darkness, but it should not be coming at us from those who are in the Kingdom of Jesus Christ. Too many times, I have heard from the pulpit, from preachers and other renowned speakers: "so what if you've been hurt, so what if you've been raped or molested, so what if somebody hurt you, stop having your pity parties and grow up." The victim is not a "so what" but an individual who has experienced great tremors to her person and has never been able to talk about it. Even if she talked about it, she was either disbelieved, blamed, or sent away and told to forget about it, to bear the burden alone without proper healing and follow—up.

How different it would be if those who make these remarks were in these sisters' shoes. Then they would want everybody to pray for them, come to their rescue and mop up their tears because they are leaders or someone who feels so indispensable to God. They will tell you real quickly, "do not touch God's anointed." Well, these sisters are also God's anointed. I have discovered that most individuals who make these remarks have never experienced your pain or either they have recovered from their own pain, and forgot that they are now supposed to strengthen the brethren! Therefore, a sister's pain is "so what" to them.

This is "no pity party", but a reality, something that is burned in one's brain and soul. To have one's person invaded and forcibly pounced upon is not a "so what". Each one of us has experienced pain in one way or another, some much more severe than others. Therefore, since we are each different, with different make—ups and different emotions, what might be considered a "so what" to one person is not a "so what" to another. It could be the breaking point to suicide.

So many of God's people "are weary in well doing" for one reason or another because there seems to be no end to the fight to stay on top. Others find themselves falling from the grace and peace of God;

they feel hopeless, helpless, depressed, despondent, frustrated, angry, upset, manipulated, used, devastated, dejected, and rejected — YET, WE FINGER POINT AND CONDEMN!

Yes, there is a groaning of burden, even as Hannah, whose womb had been shut up by God, and her enemy, Peninnah, was left to torment, vex, and aggravate Hannah, causing bitterness of soul and sore weeping. Even when she went into the temple to pour out her soul before God who was her only solution, she was grossly misunderstood by the very one who should have been spiritually alert, and that was the man of God, the priest, Eli.

YES . . . . . YES

These saints come to the house of God, raise their hands at command (as I did), sing praise songs (as I did), felt like "flying" away for a moment, a few days or hours (as I did), but what takes place after that... ?

The devil (satan), that deceiver, that liar, that murderer, that accuser, that thief, the embezzler comes along with his demons and tries to defeat us in our feelings, and hits us where we are the most vulnerable. He hits us over and over again in those places that we thought were healed. There is a scab growing over the wound, but underneath it is raw and has become infected. He brings up the past and keeps us in the present, and dares us to move on to the future – the tomorrow! He keeps us walking around in the circle of religion where we cannot move on to the fullness of salvation, since salvation is that transforming power of Jesus Christ, which He obtained by His death, burial, and resurrection; whereby, He redeemed us from the curse of the law and the dominion of sin. Salvation causes the past to be null and void if we are willing to appropriate the victory of Jesus Christ, wherein we can move from glory to glory.

The religious circle demands that we always look good, act good, be good, and never ever let anyone know that I don't have it all together, naturally or spiritually. Never ever say:

- I have not really forgiven nor forgotten; there is still bitterness inside. I can't stop hurting; I don't know how to deal with this spirit of unforgiveness, jealousy, anger, fear, rage, and resentment.
- All these crazy things and thoughts continue to move in and out of my mind and body, even when I am asleep.
- Sometimes the inner pain and feelings are so deep that I cannot myself identify them; I am even ashamed and afraid to confess my lack and insufficiency to God, let alone letting God's people know how I feel because they will accuse me of having a pity–party.

Religion will not let me be honest, but Salvation says that I can come without money or price to the fountain of life and have my thirsty soul cleansed and refreshed; I can buy wine and milk, which brings health to my soul, mind, and body without a price (Is. 55:1). In Salvation, I am not despised if my heart and spirit are broken and contrite (Ps. 34:18). Salvation is Jesus, for He healeth the broken in heart, and bindeth up their wounds (Ps. 147:3; Is. 61:1–3). Salvation says that I can come boldly to the throne of God and there I can obtain mercy and grace to help in the time of need (Heb. 4:16).

Salvation does not specialize in making the outside of the cup look wonderful, lovely, and good, but the Holy Spirit specializes in cleaning the inside of the cup from all filthiness and germs, bringing about "Internal Holiness and Wholeness" — better known as "Inner Healing." Praise God, there is a Balm in Gilead!

I can hear some of those who are reading this book saying, "if those women were really saved, they would not be feeling like this, they would always have victory." Well, they do have victory because Jesus is much alive and well, and He is always available to deal with those things that concern us, no matter what they are. We belong to Him and Him only, and one soul is as important to Him as a thousand — PRAISE GOD!!

DON'T WORRY ABOUT THE "FINGER–POINTERS" OR THE CONDEMNERS, OR THE "MOCKERS", MOVE TO HIGHER GROUNDS WHERE THE HEALER OF healers DWELLS, – JESUS CHRIST!!!

THE GAME OF PRETENSE

Many of the injured and wounded came into salvation after their dreams were shattered or were already in when their dreams were shattered. We were told and are still being told that if we praise God, get involved in various church activities, pray, fast, and do all the other things that the church requires everything will be alright. There will be no more hurts or pain and all our troubles will be over. To act in any other way or say differently means that you do not have faith; you are not saved or you are in rebellion.

So, we put up a big, big, enormous front to please people, pretending that we've got it all together. We flounce around with lots of green leaves but no fruit. The most pathetic thing is that we know that we don't have any fruit — Let's be real! When someone asks how we are doing, we mechanically spit—out, "I'm blessed." Yes, you are blessed, but you really don't know it because to truly know that you are blessed means that the front can come down, down, down! You do not have to put on a false face with God nor man. The mask can come off, Amen!

To cry out for help means that you are having a pity—party or you are told to forget it, push it back, ignore it, don't mention it. Don't dare say that you are having sexual problems, so much so that your sleep is disturbed, and that you feel like climbing up a wall, along with all the other emotional tremors that comes with the territory. To acknowledge that these things exist, one is condemned, even by those who are having the same problems but are afraid to admit it. They want the church and other people to believe that they are more righteous than you, and that they have always had it all together. They would not dare take the time to look into your eyes and recognize the pain and hurt in your heart, for to look means that they will see themselves.

Yes, you know that you love God and want to please Him and have tried to put on a happy face, but deep, deep, down inside the hurt is real. You are angry with the one who hurt you, angry with yourself, and with God. Not only are you angry, but you feel like a fool, totally betrayed. It seems that God did not hear you, and you wonder why did He let this happen to you anyway: "Could not He have stopped the childhood abuse?" Could not He have stopped the one you loved from betraying you? Could not He have stopped your marriage from falling to pieces or your husband from dying? "Why can't He give me the peace I need? I have cried over and over again, and I have done all those things that the saints told me to do. I have been from one revival to another revival, from one prophet to another trying to find the answer, yet the pain has not left." The question still rings out... why, why, why? For years, I asked some of these same questions, why, why, why!

For many, the hurt and pain have frozen them up on the inside. For others, there is a silent cry coming forth out of their eyes saying, "Doesn't someone see me, it's just me that wanted to be discovered, loved and held. It's me that wanted to be placed in the security of someone who would have understood me, loved me, protected me, and fulfilled my dream. Will it ever happen or why didn't it happen"? No one knows the loneliness, the pain, and the times these women have agonized, saying: "I <u>do</u> want to love again, but I am afraid to open up and trust, really trust again. <u>The fire has burned me</u>."

After the activities of the day end, you lie down in bed trying to rest because you are so fatigued but cannot sleep. There is something missing. What is it? Is it the real you trying to get out into the reality of your true needs? Is it the real you, that girl spirit who is now grown, trying to get free? Is it the real you who has been imprisoned and immobilized from the years of brokennes, hardness, and "a don't care and don't want to be bothered" attitude? You can't trust, you are devastated and you have open wounds which you thought were healed, but someone or something always digs into them again and again.

The memory of it all is more than you can stand; but above all, you can't forget nor forgive because there are layers and layers of hurts and rubbish — oh, the loneliness. You are very vulnerable, so you cover yourself well. You fake a smile and fake a strut, but deep down inside you hear The Spirit of God saying over and over again:

> "Be free, be free. Freedom is your life–line to
> wholeness, to living again. Freedom from what people
> think or say about you. It is what I want for you, and

what I want you to think of yourself. You are fearfully
and wonderfully made; I created you and I know you
all together."

Oh, my, you hear it over and over again, but do not have the ability to respond. You feel dead inside.

There are some things we will never understand, nor can they be put into any particular order, but the questions that must be confronted or that you must come face to face with are:

- Do I need to be healed from the past once and for all?

- Do I really want to be healed?

- Can I be healed?

- Who or what can heal me?

- Where can I go for that healing?

- How long will it take?

In the physical aspect, many people have suffered severe pain and diseases for so long that they have resigned themselves to live this way. They take pain killers, after pain killers, after pain killers and ignore the fact that there are hospitals, clinics, and doctors who are available to diagnose, treat, and begin the healing process. Their condition becomes so severe that it is life threatening, often leaving people cripples, invalids or severely diseased. They passively suffer without resistance, never free from pain or disease until it is finally too late, and they die. They never lived life to its fullest.

To acknowledge that a condition exists is wonderful, for it can be the beginning of the possible healing process; however, if one never gets up and goes for the help or necessary treatments, one will never be healed. The possibility of recovery is then null and void.

If one is able to acknowledge one's sickness, whether physical or psychological, and finally go for diagnosis and prescribed treatments, one then must follow through with the doctor's orders. Just because one begins to feel better, this does not mean that one should stop the treatments but must continue to have check—ups on a regular basis to be certain that there is no reoccurrence of the previous condition, and that there can be an early detection if anything new occurs.

Many of us in the spiritual realm are as those with physical and psychological sicknesses mentioned above. We have such deep seated bitterness and pain from the past that we have carried them over into the present. We have shouted, hollered, cried, given smiles of pretense, sat with the saints but feel like we really do not belong. We have overdressed, underdressed, rebuked satan, pleaded the blood, laid awake at night, suffered stomach ulcers, nerves shot, workaholics, never relaxed, afraid to say no to every demand made upon us by the church, friends, and children for fear of further rejection and disapproval. We are never fulfilled as a woman, let alone as the woman of God.

Jesus said in Mt. 9:12, "They that be whole need not a physician, but they that are sick." If you are sick in mind, body, soul or spirit, you need to be healed!! Jesus is the Chief Physician who can heal all manner of diseases, whether it is body, soul or spirit, or whether it is past or present. Stop looking in satan's crystal ball to see what your future will be, but look into the face of Jesus who not only knows the future, but He holds the entire world and its future in His hands. That includes you and me. Only Jesus knows what tomorrow holds.

When we were children if we hurt ourselves, our mother or father would kiss the place where we hurt, giving us comfort that the pain was gone when it actually had not. We got up and dusted ourselves off and pretended that it did not hurt even though we had scars and bruises which needed to be treated.

I remember that as a child I experienced bad ear aches which would cause me to cry. My mother would let my cousin, Joe, blow smoke into my ear from his pipe and put a few drops of sweet oil in the ear. This was to have cured the ear ache, and I dared not say that I still had the pain for fear of a scolding or a beating. I would go away to play holding my ears pretending that everything was alright. If I played hard enough and became absorbed in something else, I would forget the pain, but it was still there and repeatedly returned. Oh, yes, the pipe smoke and the sweet oil may have given temporary relief, but it never got to the root of the problem which would have saved my hearing. Today, I have 85% hearing loss in both ears.

I do not care how many artificial remedies one uses, or how many kisses you get, or how many sweet little words are said, but, they will not get to the root cause of your pain and hurt. Mother, father, sister, brother or anyone else can't kiss this pain, hurt, anger, or unforgiveness away. Yes, you have played hard at pretense; In fact, you have almost become a professional pretender. Satan knows how to make us actresses, and we fall for his sales pitch, and buy his ware. Aren't you sick of pretending?

The root cause is still there because it continues to resurface, and resurface and resurface over and over again. It must be dug out by the roots by the one who knows how to get to the root of things, and that is God Himself. Who would know better than God since He created every bone, nerve, cell, and tissue in our being. He even created our eyes so that they can shed tears and gave us hearts to feel emotions. Since He put us together and knows every fiber of our being, He knows exactly where to find those broken, torn, and defected places and install brand new parts. He is so skillful and all knowing that He knows exactly what to do and when to do it. He knows exactly how long the surgery will take, and whether it should all be done in one setting or in intervals. What a Mighty God is our God. He is the only wise God, the God who sees and knows all things – The God that does not sleep or slumber.

Yes, <u>Inner Healing Is Painful</u> because there are so many layers which must be cut away – No, we cannot praise our way out of this. The price of change is costly because you must leave your comfort zone and familiarity where satan has had you living, and has made you believe that there is no hope by causing your vision to be impaired. He has kept a cloudy fog screen over who and what God has made you to be, and what your potentials are in and through the Living God. This impairment has stunned your growth both naturally, spiritually, and emotionally.

You must admit or acknowledge that you need to be healed and delivered from those things that have a stronghold over your mind, heart, emotions, and soul. There will and must be extensive surgery performed by the skillful hands of the Chief Surgeon, the Great Physician, the I Am, Jesus Christ. He is a specialist in creating new hearts and replacing right spirits. The inner man must be restored and refurbished. Therefore, you must be taken back to the potter's house to be put back on the wheel. Your life is at stake and your womb is barren. ARE YOU WILLING TO GO

MY JOURNEY TO THE PIG'S PEN

There are those of you who have experienced such great, great, traumatic experiences in your life that it would very difficult for me to even compare my testimony to yours, but the one thing that I have learned is that pain is pain no matter how it happened, especially when it has almost taken you to the "pit of hell." Therefore, I want to share with you just a brief account of what I call "My Journey to the Pig's Pen." The circumstances of that journey wrought much pain, hurt, disappointments and near devastation before I could come to myself. With the help of God, I have moved to the life of wholeness.

The story of my beginning and what really brought a change in my life is so enormous that it would take pages and pages to write about them, if I ever could. There were some emotions and experiences that occurred in my life that I could never express in writing or define them myself. Yet, it is so interesting how others have tried to tell my story, especially the 8 years of entrapment in the pig's pen, but they do not even know the story or the whole truth of the matter. Therefore, I want to share just a small portion with you, and pray that you will understand why I understand pain, even though it might not be the same as yours. Above all, I pray that you will understand that you can be healed from hurt and pain no matter how hard it is or no matter how long you have been in your pain.

It is so interesting how vulnerable I was when I was looking for love, fulfillment, and "the who I was" in order to stop the inner pain, hurts, and confusion of my life. I was so vulnerable because I had no experience with life or living except the experiences of pain, hurts, and disappointments. As I reflect back on my life from childhood, adolescence, teenage, early adulthood, and even my late thirties, I wrestled so long with very, very low self–esteem, broken relationships, and a great feeling of inferiority and guilt. I did not know who I was, nor where I was going. I made many bad choices and settled for many wrong things because I was searching for love and self–identity from anyone or anything.

Yes, anyone or anything that could ease the pain and hurts that had stabbed my heart at childhood. I wanted someone to help me get rid of the hollow in my soul and heart and help me to find the real me who was buried so deep inside. I needed someone to help me fulfill my dreams and find my destiny. But in the course of my search, I was damaged even more.

I was really a very unhappy person most of my life until I reached 40 years old. My life was made up of pain, hurts on top of hurts, disappointments, extreme anger, bitterness, and frustration, coupled with very low self–esteem. Most of my developmental years, I was called ugly, dumb, stupid, black (I a was very dark complexion), "fatso" and other derogatory names. My classmates and people who I did not even know would laugh and make fun of me. One day I was going on an errand for my mother, and while waiting on the corner for the street car, a group of complete strangers passed by in a car and called me all kinds of nasty and foul names. How embarrassed and hurt I was. This is when I learned that people could be so cruel.

I believed that life would have been different for me if I had a father to protect me and be there for me, but my father died when I was 9 years old. I only have fond memories of my dad, whom I resemble so much. My father was blind, but I remember taking him for walks in the neighborhood. We laughed and I would talked with him as a small child does while we walked or when I came home from school. He was such a kind, gentle dad.

Well, it was a very different story with my mother. She treated me like a servant instead of a daughter. While I was down on my knees scrubbing floors, or washing clothes on a scrub board, or chopping wood, sifting cinders (chunks of burned coal), or moving furniture, she was constantly fussing, complaining, and finding fault, demanding more and more. My sibling, who was the oldest, was out playing with boys and was never required to do much of anything. I had holes in my shoes and wore clothing of inferior quality and quantity because my sibling was given special attention and first priority. She was my mother's doll baby.

I never remembered my mother ever hugging me or telling me that she loved me, nor giving me affection or reassurance. It was only on her death bed that she looked up and said, "I never knew what I had in a daughter until now" — it was too late then! Two days later, she died; it was on Mother's Day. I often wonder what it would be like now if she was alive today.

I was constantly beaten with belts, sticks, ironing cords, ropes, shoes, or anything my mother could put her hands on. I was beaten for the least little thing, especially if I tried to express myself. I was called "sassy", rebellious, belligerent or a stubborn mule, and many other names. I am not sure why my mother treated me so differently, but I now know that I was different in a positive way, even though I could only generate a negative attitude at that time due to abuse. I am glad that I was and am different because I was determined to survive no matter what happened to me. Determination is very, very important for survival, or you will "crack-up"!!

One of the incidents that always sticks out in my mind is my graduation in 1952. In the fifties we graduated in evening gowns, but when I told my mother what I needed for my graduation, she said that she had no money to buy a gown and that I just would not walk with my class. The next day when I went to school, my Biology Teacher, Mrs. Bishop asked me was I ready for graduation because she was proud of the change in me. I told her that I would not be able to walk with the class because my mother did not have the money to buy me a gown. Mrs. Bishop, who had been such an encouragement to me as I struggled to finish high school, contacted several teachers who contributed to the purchase of my gown.

I came home so excited with this pretty wrapped box containing my gown, only to be accused of letting some man buy my gown. I could not understand this because I was not even thinking about a man at that time, nor did I have a boyfriend. When I tried to defend myself and explain where the gown came from and who bought it, my mother told me to shut up because I was lying. She beat me so severely and took the gown and threw it in the corner. She never tried to find out the truth of what I told her. Not only did my body hurt, but my heart was hurt and crushed.

When I went to school a couple of days later with a wounded spirit and wounds on my body, I told Mrs. Bishop what had happened. She went home with me after school to verify that I was telling the truth; only then was I allowed to keep the gown. My mother never apologized or said she was sorry (mothers have such a vast impact on their children's success or failure in life). I did graduate from high school and later became employed as a nurse's aide, earning $27.50 weekly. I was only allowed to keep $5.00 of my earnings because my mother took the balance, and I had no say in the matter.

In the process of it all, it was not just the wounds inflicted upon my body and mind by my mother and others which left me with no self–worth, but the wounds that I inflicted upon myself through the constant feeling of inferiority. I felt that I was not like other girls nor could be, even though I longed to be. I only saw myself as they had painted me: dumb, ugly, stupid, black, and fat. I felt that I was of no worth to God, myself or anyone else. Yes, I had teenage friends in the church, but I was not able to properly relate to them because I was not really sure if some of them were really my friends because of some of the things that they said to me. As a result of all this, I became very, very hard, bitter, angry, and mean. My fist and tongue became a powerful weapon for me to defend myself against anyone that I felt was hurting me or was about to hurt me, be it male or female.

I fought constantly through my childhood and teen years, hurting others as I was hurting, even if they had done nothing to me. I was such a very lonely, rejected person. Occasionally, I would have fun and laugh, but most of the time, I was on the defensive. Even in my childhood, I asked God so often to help me, rescue me, free me, and send someone in my life to discover the real me, as so many of you have asked God. The real me was so full of love which I really wanted to give to someone, but it was buried so deep under the anger, hardness, bitterness, and the feeling of nothingness. Over and over, I dreamed and wanted to be like other girls, but I did not know how to.

I was filled with the Holy Spirit at 9 years old, but I did not know how to appreciate God's love because I was too young and immature to be aware of what it was, nor did I know how to appropriate this wonderful salvation. I really did not understand the love of God as I do today. We were never taught much about His love. We sang, "Yes Jesus love me because the Bible tells me so", but the emphasis was not placed on love but on the does and don'ts, the rules and regulations, the going to hell if you did the least thing wrong, and the sternness of always being pure and righteous.

Now, I can agree with the Apostle Paul when he said, "when I was a child, I spake as a child, I understood as a child, I thought as a child: but when I became a man, I put away childish things" (I Co. 13:11). No, I had no wisdom or understanding of how to cope with life at that point because I really was a crippled child, full of anger and bitterness.

At the age of 18 years old, I met the man whom I thought was my "Mr. Right", my Knight in Shining Armor". He was 10 years older than I, tall, good looking, handsome, and a sharp dresser. How intrigued I was with this man. He was walking just the right walk and talking just the right talk. He was not in church nor did he confess salvation. How my heart opened up because of his sweet words which I had never heard before.

One night he invited me out to meet his father and step—mother after we had known each other for about six months; But my mother forbade me to go. She told me that if I went out that night not to ever come back to her house. I was willing to take the risk, not just to get away from my mother's home, but above all to be loved, as I thought. Yes, I was willing to leave the little that I knew in order to receive and give love. I walked away from my mother's home never to return for 8 years. I now look back at this and laugh because I did not realize how crazy and stupid this was... IT WAS A TERRIBLE, TERRIBLE, TERRIBLE DECISION!!! Today, I can warn other young girls not to take the path I took because it will only lead to much heartache and pain!! We must learn by others' mistakes and not seek to get our own experience of pain. If I fell into a ditch and severely injured myself, why should you go the same path and fall into the same ditch. But somehow, so many feel that I can take that path and nothing will happen to me; if we would only listen! Many times, I wished that I would have listened.

Luke 15:11–14 tells the account of a father who had two sons. The younger son, who was later called the prodigal son, asked his father for his inheritance, left his father's house, went to a foreign (far) country and wasted his substance with riotous living. When he had spent all, there arose a mighty famine in the land, and he began to be in need.

Well, I like the prodigal son chose to walk away from my mother's home (though I had no inheritance to take), from God and the church for 8 years, not realizing that I was sending myself down a path of deeper pain, hurt, and near destruction. The very thing that I went after almost caused my death. The one thing I know, now, is that satan will make things look so wonderful until he gets you on his territory, and then he will try to kill you. For a while my life away from home satisfied, but it did not last long because the pleasure of sin is but for a season.

I was constantly abused physically and mentally, suffering much trauma to my person. I was hospitalized on several occasions due to contagious diseases which he brought home to me. My youngest daughter was supposed to be born blind from the last disease I contacted, but thank God for His mercy; she was not born blind! In spite of it all, I still tried to make the relationship work at the expense of my life and that of my children. I lived in a state of constant fear and rejection, feeling abandoned by those whom I thought cared about me a little. But, somewhere deep down inside, I knew that God had not forsaken me, nor had He abandoned me. However, He had to send a famine in my life to make me come to myself - how He loves us!

This one occasion will always stay with me, and it will always attest to the fact that God had not forsaken me even in my sins and my turning away from His presence: One night my Knight and I went to my girlfriend's prom, but before long, we became involved in a heated argument. He became so upset and enraged and threatened to kill me rather than for anyone else to have me, all because some of the guys who were my former classmates were there and we began to talk and "cut–up" with one another.

When we finally got home that night (we only had a room), I went upstairs to our room while he stayed downstairs where our landlord was having a party. I fell asleep quickly since I was 4 months pregnant. I know it was God who woke me up because it was as if someone had shaken me. When I awoke the bed was on fire, burning rapidly. He was sitting there looking at me waiting for me to burn up. He said, "I told you that I would kill you". I was so afraid, I began to scream and holler. There was only one way out of the bed because the bed was against the wall, and that was to climb over the foot board which was made of metal. I heard the voice of God say, "climb over, it will not burn you." I climbed over that metal foot board which had become extremely hot, but I was not burned or scorched. God helped me to escape death... Hallelujah!!

My screams and the smell of the smoke awoke our landlord, who called the fire department to extinguish the flames. Of course, we had to move as we had to do so many other times. I look back now and praise and worship God with all my heart for His abundant mercies, longsuffering and love because I could have been destroyed. I could have died without having a chance to be reconciled to my Father, Jesus Christ. People can say what they may, but I am a living witness that God does continually deal with us even in our mess, or in our deepest valley of despair because He wishes that we be restored unto Him (the whole person) and not perish!

After a short separation from my mate, we reconciled because my heart was still involved and I thought perhaps he would change. By this time, we had two daughters and we moved to Durham, North Carolina with his grandparents. These were the better days of our life together. His grandparents were very elderly and believed in the old—fashioned way of marriage and how a woman should be treated by a man. His grandfather dared him to even raise his voice at me, much less hit me. These were times of contentment, but there still was a missing link. There was a void and feeling of aloneness and sadness all the time.

For two years, I had not had any contact with my mother, sister or anyone that I knew from the past. Early one Sunday morning, I was up fixing breakfast when a knock came on the back door. I opened the door and there stood my mother and my little nephew. I was so shocked and surprised. In spite of all that had happened in the past, I was so glad to see my mother. I invited her in, but she refused. There I stood with the door open, continually inviting her in, but she looked me square in the face and she said, "I only came down here to tell you that God will never forgive you." At that, she turned around and walked away. Oh, how this cut so very, very deep into my heart and spirit. I knew that I was living in sin, away from the fellowship of God and my church family, but to think that God would never forgive me was so very devastating. After that I lived with more fear, constant guilt, and additional shame. I was a total mess!

I can assuredly say with the scripture recorded in Ps. 27:10: "When my father and my mother forsake me, then the Lord will take you up." God has so many numerous ways of proving himself to us. He has a way of <u>causing</u> us to yield, even though it is in His power to <u>make</u> us yield since He is Sovereign. God wants us to come to our senses and return to our Father's house because of His love for us and our need for Him.

After returning to Baltimore, the fighting and the abuse resumed again; in fact, it got worse. It got to the place that it was nothing strange to come home and find a woman in my bed. Sex was forced on me or men were brought home for me to prostitute myself with, which I absolutely refused to do so. My refusal enraged him the more causing more severe beatings. The money that I earned as a domestic worker was demanded and taken by force if I did not give it to him. Oh, yes, I stayed, still thinking that I could change the situation — how very foolish!

I wanted to leave, but I was afraid! I was always wondering where would I go and how I would take care of my two small children? It is so interesting how fear will not allow you to think straight; it paralyzes you! It is no wonder the Bible indicates that fear not only brings us into bondage, but it also brings torment. As a result, many days we had no food, milk or clothing. Only by the mercy of God, and the kindness of a family that I worked for was I able to feed my children. Often, I would be desperately in need, so I would humble myself and ask my mother for food or money, but she refused me every time. She would tell me: "you made your bed hard, now lay on it."

Here I was with hardly anything, and I was taking care of my children anyway with the little money I earned ($2.00 per day) and with the aid of my employer, but there I sat wondering where I would go and how I would support my children. It was my fear, yes, but it was also because my heart was still involved. Yes, I was afraid, but fear was now turning into hate, more anger, and more bitterness. My childhood loomed before me so very often, and I realized that the two persons whom I trusted with my life, and who should have loved me did not, they both abused me — I now felt hate for both of them.

One night I had a dream that there were Roman soldiers going out to kill everyone that they could find; however, if you could get to this large city, you would be saved. As I started to run to this city, I remembered my family. I ran back toward our home to get my family, but soldiers were approaching, so I ran and hid under this bridge. I heard a voice saying, "SAVE YOURSELF." As soon as the soldiers passed over, I turned and ran as fast as I could back toward that city which resembled a huge castle with a drawbridge. As soon as my feet got on the drawbridge, the drawbridge began to close, and I slid down into the city and I was safe.

Luke 15:15–16 (NRSV) gives this further account of the prodigal son: "So he went and hired himself to a citizen of that country, who sent him to his field to feed the pigs. He would gladly have filled himself with the pod that the pigs were eating, and no one gave him anything."

I knew God was calling me to return to Him, but I was too ashamed. I did not have the strength to get up and to return, even though I was deep down in the "pigs' pen", dirty, ragged, torn, very angry, and full of fear. I felt too helpless and hopeless to escape the trap that I had allowed satan to ensnare me in.

A few days after this dream, a knock came on my apartment door and when I opened the door there stood one of the beloved mothers of my church, Mother Geneva Watson (Mom Nee), who is now deceased. My first thoughts were, "here comes another one of the saints to preach to me and to tell me how wrong I was" (I had many of those visitors). I knew that I was wrong and out of God's will, so I did not want to hear it over and over again from anyone; but this loving mother said, "I just came to tell you how much I love you and that God loves you too." I fell into her arms and began to cry and weep like a baby!! I could hear the voice of God in this beloved servant who came not to preach, nor to tell me how wrong I was. She came to seek that lost sheep, just as Jesus left the 99 sheep in the fold to find the one lost sheep... ME!!!! God knew how to send me help just in time.

The "straw that broke the camel's back" and which almost made me a murderer, occurred one night when "Mr. Wrong" (note: the name has now changed) told me he was going out that night in spite of our children being sick. I asked him to stay home and help me with the children because I was tired after scrubbing and working hard at my job. Of course, he refused. Before he left the apartment, he began to curse at me and became very irritated during our conversation. He slapped me in my face and hit me in my eye very hard which caused me to bleed, leaving a deep cut over the eye. He slammed out of the apartment not caring what he had done to me. I went to the window after he went down the stairs only to see him join another woman who was waiting for him across the street.

I sat in the chair feeling totally dead inside. While sitting in that chair for hours unable to move, the years of fear lifted and anger turned into rage. I began to realize that this had been a one–sided love, and I could not make him love me no matter how hard I tried or what I did. I had given so much of what I had; in fact, all I had!! I now despised him, and he had to pay for the abuse that he had inflicted on my body, my mind, and my very soul for almost 8 years!!

I felt my mind snap, and I no longer cared. Satan began to feed my mind with "he must die, you must kill him". Satan gave me specific instructions how to kill him. Believe me, satan takes everything you have and destroys you from without and from within. The scripture is so very true when it says that satan comes to steal, kill and destroy. Hate had now turned into rage, with the desire to kill. Not only was I now willing to destroy him, but also myself in the process.

Per instructions from satan who was now in control: I put a large pot of water on the stove to boil, which I kept replenished and boiling with a hammer by my side. I was instructed to throw the boiling water in his face to scald and blind him when he came through the door, and then beat him in the head with the hammer after pouring the scalding water on him. About 1:30 a.m. when he did not come home, I left my children at home asleep, and I walked frantically, with double strength and fearlessness, to every bar and night club that I knew he frequented with a straight razor in my pocket to cut him to death, but I could not find him. I was like a mad woman; I was in a state of insanity. No sleep came to my eyes until about 6:30 a.m. that next morning. When I awoke about 11:30 a.m., I began to realize that God had prevented me from being a murderer, and I had to leave now, not tomorrow, but now. GOD HAD PREVENTED THE PLAN OF satan, HALLELUJAH!!!

I began to pack my trunk, which I knew that I could not take at that moment. So I put just enough clothes for myself and my children in a paper bag that I could easily carry, which was not much because we had very little. While I was packing, he came in and tried to stop me, but there was no stopping now. I left this time and never returned (that has been over 45 years ago). My sister took us in. It was a few months later that I learned that he was in a house about three doors from where we lived the night that I went out to kill him.

I thank God each and every day for stopping satan's plan to destroy me, and I thank Him that I did not take a life. I learned how the wrong love and the wrong involvement, no matter how wonderful it seems, can turn into bitterness and bitterness turns to hate, and hate turns to rage and rage produces destruction of oneself and others. **If only we would remove and separate ourselves from wrong death–like situations before bitterness and rage set in...** I OWE GOD SO MUCH!! WHAT ABOUT YOU?

BACK TO THE FATHER FOR CHANGE

"<u>When he came to himself</u>, he said, how many servants of my father's have bread enough to spare and I perish with hunger! I will say unto him, Father, I have sinned against heaven, and before thee, And am no more worthy to be called thy son: make me as one of your hired servants. <u>And he arose and came to his father</u>. But when he was yet a great way off, his father saw him and had compassion, and ran, and fell on his neck, and kissed him. And the son said unto him, father, I have sinned against heaven, and in thy sight, and no more worthy to be called thy son. But the father said to his servants, bring forth the best robe, and put it on him; and put a ring on his hand, and shoes on his feet: And bring hither the fatted calf, and kill it; and let us eat, and be merry. For this my son was dead, and is alive again; he was lost, and is found. And they began to make merry." Luke 15:17–24 (KJV)

I came to myself down in the pigs' pen! I was wasted, worn, torn, and desperate for a cleansing and a surge of new life! I was actually dead inside and outside. I needed help badly. Not human help necessarily, but the kind of help that only God could give. Two weeks after leaving the pigs pen, I got up enough courage to go back to my home church on Sunday night. A few of the saints greeted me warmly, but others were very distant and cold toward me. It took all that I had to sit through the service because I was embarrassed and ashamed, and I again felt rejection from the people of God, those that I used to walk with. When the altar call was made, I wanted to go forth, but I was so ashamed and my mother was looking at me with hatred and a pious look.

God, our Father is such a forgiving and merciful God. You can come as you are: messed up, cotton dress (which I had on), no money, and no future in sight, battle scars, cast down and feeling low as the ground, but He will not cast you away. He will welcome you back with open arms because He has been waiting and looking for His son (Me), all the time. God views every sinner not as just a mere possession, but he views us with compassion as a person worthy of His love; He not only views us as a son who was lost, but as one whom He loved and longed for his return. God desires that each one return to him. What a magnificent and marvelous Father and Friend that sticks closer than a brother!!!!

When the altar call was made, I sat there glued to my seat wanting to make my way to the altar, but I was so embarrassed. The Holy Spirit took me by my arms, lifted me from my seat and before I knew it, I was at the altar crying and telling God how sorry I was for all that I had done and how I had hurt Him. No, the saints did not welcome me with open arms, but my Abba Father did because He knew my heart. I am so glad that God is not like people, Praise God!!!

For a very long time, I was not accepted by the church and when I tried to tell one sister how God dealt with me while I was out of the church, she looked at me and said that it was not true because God does not hear a sinner pray (a misinterpretation of scripture). I did not have to argue with her because I knew that God did hear my prayers and visited with me while I was away from His fellowship; He was waiting for me to come to myself.

No, not all of the tremors of those past 8 years had been left at the altar. I still had the pain, scars, bruises, and hatred to deal with. It was no longer just myself to deal with, but I now had two beautiful daughters to raise. I had to help them to be healed from the abusive situation in which we lived, especially one daughter who was terribly affected by the abuse. However, the empty place in my heart was yet crying out for fulfillment, the need to give and receive.

Things went well for a while, but my sexual desires soon kicked—in and caused me to become restless and feel out—of—control. I again had the desire to search for love, acceptance, and someone to help me to heal. I guess you are saying, didn't she go through enough for 8 years. Yes, I did, but it is so hard to explain how human emotions work. They are like an empty hole that should have been filled, but had not; therefore, I was still searching for that which would fill it or satisfy its emptiness. It is also like a person who is hungry and who eats one thing after another to satisfy his taste buds, when most often it is the most simple, small thing that satisfies that taste.

Yes, even after my first trip to the altar, I was still hurting and in pain, but I got involved in several short—term relationships again.

Therefore, I can only say that the love and mercy of God was greater and stronger than my sins. I can unequivocally agree that: "Love is stronger than death" (S of S 8:6, 7), and "Love does cover a multitude of sin" (Pr. 10:12; I Pe. 4:8). God's love is a perfect love which no human being, no matter who they are, has yet been able to fully comprehend or fathom!! There is a song that ask the question: "Who can fathom the depth of His love? I stand, I stand in awe of you Holy God to whom all praises due... Talking about "Tough Love", this is it!! Today, I stand in awe of this mighty God. I am always amazed at how He works!

Praise God, His mercy endures forever. In spite of me, the Lord eventually blessed me with a good job and a nice apartment in public housing where the rent was affordable. No, I am not trying to justify my sins by God's mercy, nor am I trying to make an excuse for my mess, I am only giving my testimony as it was. THANK GOD IT IS NOT LIKE THAT TODAY!!! GOD CHANGED ME FROM THE INSIDE OUT!!

After the Lord blessed me with a decent job and salary, I began to spend lots of money traveling all over the country and entertaining lots and lots of people in my home, only to discover that these things really did not satisfy, nor did they have the power to break the vicious cycle which was like a dark cloud still hanging over my life. I could not get away from me because everything that I did and everywhere I went, the "me" loomed before my face, the rottenness, "the me that nobody knew" but myself and God. Some of me which I thought I knew, it took God to reveal that I really did not know me altogether, only He knew! I remember the last time that I traveled to California for vacation "to get away"; I heard the voice of God say, "You can't get away from yourself nor from me because you carry you with you, and I am present everywhere.

I can say with a cloud of other witnesses, that there can never be, nor are there any "quick fixes". If we do not lose the very taste for our imprisonment, the rottenness that has left a foul taste in our mouth, "the down—in—the —dog feeling", we will remain where we are. Just like people addicted to drugs, no matter how many programs they go to, or no matter how many times they are sent to various institutions to dry—out or kick the habit, if they do not lose their taste for drugs, they will return back to the old habit and the life of enslavement.

As women, we will never leave an abusive, sick relationship, whether it be physical, mental or no matter how often it occurs, be it weeks, months or years, as long as our heart is involved. When we get sick and tired of being abused and the element of fear is removed, only then will we decide to fight for our freedom. As many pep talks and advice as we may receive, we will go back every time if we are not really sick and tired. This same principle applies to any situation in our life that has us bound, tied up and imprisoned.

Yes, we must get sick of ourselves! We must get sick of the stink! We must get sick and tired of being sick and tired! We must finally get sick of putting up a front because the least strong wind that blows will expose the real us. To only look good on the outside is worthless (Hey, by the way, some don't even look good on the outside. The slip is showing, the heels are all turned over, and the lipstick is on crooked). But above all, we will never produce the kind of fruit that Jesus desires to eat when He passes by. That's how I was, no fruit.

The tree then must be cursed at the root (read Mt. 21:17–21). It was not that the fig tree was not a fig tree, or that it did not have

49

beautiful leaves, the problem was that it was growing against nature, not fulfilling the purpose that God created it for. Its purpose was to produce fruit first for a life sustaining purpose and afterward leaves for protection of the fruit, and finally its purpose was for beauty. This thing in me had to be cursed and destroyed at the roots — the enslavement of my flesh had to die!!

Because we were created to bear fruit and be productive, that poisonous thing call unforgiveness, hatred, bitterness, anger, depression, hopelessness, helplessness, despair, low self—esteem, will kill the ability that God placed within us to bring forth fruit. It will cause us to be sterile. These elements have a contrary nature against God and a mind of their own. They are lawless, lewd, destructive and will take total control of every part of us.

The fence or wall must be torn down piece by piece! It can't just be torn down or just cut it off at the top, but the ground must be dug up and the axe laid to the root foundation and burned up. As a tree, if it is not dealt with at the root and the stump dug—up, it will spring up again, often producing more negative effects.

Oh, How I know!! Much of what I was or what I was doing after I returned to the church no one knew. I put up a big, bad front; I kept a chip on my shoulder and knew how to defend myself if anyone dared to infringe upon my territory. I covered myself well. I sang on the choir, could shout on every song and spoke with tongues, but God knew me all together. I knew that I was on my way down again. However, I was still not willing to totally surrender, laying the axe to the root of sin.

I went from one revival to another revival, from one "red—hot" church meeting to another, from one Bible class to another, from one convention to another looking for someone to give "a word" so that I could find an answer or a way to justify or to excuse the dilemma that I was in. I went to the altar week after week, month after month, year after year; I cried and cried, laid on my Bible to pray, had hands after hands laid on me, but this did not deal with the root of my problems. It was only after I got sick and tired of being sick and tired, and after I began to realize that the sins and hurt of my past were eating away at my guts, eating away at my sanity, and eating away at my relationship with God and causing me to continually live in guilt, sin, and condemnation was I able to begin recovery.

It was only then that I finally decided that once and for all that I could walk out of sin, fear, deep pain and the "couldn't help its because I am a woman", or "this is just how I am" attitude. I am now convinced that one cannot truly know God and be happy while involved in sin of any kind! Name it what you will, turn it over, try to justify it, call it little or call it big, but sin is sin and very, very displeasing to a Holy God. One might find pleasure in sin for a season, but it slowly and surely will bring death, physical, emotional or spiritual. You will be living but dead! Yes, shouting, singing, a regular church attendee, on the usher board, the deacon board, praise leader, youth leader, preacher who preaches people out of their seats and is well known all over the country, but dead, dead, dead on the inside.

We have majored in naming a few sins: smoking, drinking, fornication and adultery, but all unrighteousness is sin. We can appear as holy as we want, but sin is sin. God hates sin, and so will we when we get tired of being beat—up by the results of sin. Only when we come to ourselves as the Prodigal son, will we get up and go to our Father. Dirty and torn though we may be, but we will come. Not with pride, but seeking forgiveness, help, healing and the safety that is found only in the Father's house, and in His arms.

I was like Jacob who would not let go of the angel, but wrestled with him all night until the break of day because I was desperate for a blessing. I did not know how long my night would be, but I was guaranteed that the day would break. I might come out with a limp, but I would not only have a new name, but a new attitude and new desires.

I remember that day in 1962, standing at my ironing board preparing to take a trip to New York with a group of friends, when the state of my soul and mind overwhelmed me, causing me to fall prostrate on my face crying out to God. This was not the same cry that I had cried before, but one of total desperation. I cried out, "Lord you've got to help me, you've got to do something with me; I will not let you go until you change me." I was on the verge of madness and I could not stop crying.

I cried for hours in deep sorrow and genuine repentance before God. My soul and mind were wearied and torn. There was still an estranged relationship between God and me. Not on God's part, but mine because I was yet following Him afar off. This time, I really went searching for the One whom my soul really loved.

I know there is a saying, "we do not find God because He was never lost". This might sound wonderful, but these scriptures became real to me in those moments: "I love them that love me; and those that seek me early shall find me. For whoso findeth me findeth life, and shall obtain favor of the Lord (Pr. 8:17, 35 — KJV); And ye shall seek me, and find me, when ye search for me with all your heart" (Je. 29:13 — KJV).

No, Jesus was not lost, but I was. He told me in His Word that if I would seek after Him, He would turn away my captivity. I was in a dark hole that I could not get out of, but He became that "light which shineth more and more unto that perfect day." I saw the light, it was shining toward the hole that I was in. I began to fight and scramble to go toward that light. This time I cried out and hollered for help with all of my might, which was not much. My cry of distress caused the beacon light to turn and shine in my direction so that I could find my way to the opening of the dark tunnel. I concur with the Psalmist in Ps. 34:6: "This poor man (Delores) cried and the Lord heard her (Delores), and saved Delores from all of her distress." PRAISE GOD!!

When I came to myself, dusk had set in, I was spent, and there were no more tears to offer. I was almost too tired and weak to get up, but my mind came back to me and the refreshing breath or wind of God began to fill me.

A few days later I traveled to New York, where I attended the Institutional Church of God In Christ in Brooklyn, New York. There, God sent a mighty preacher by the name of Elder Richard Hinton from Chicago, Illinois to speak directly to me. His message was entitled, "My Son Give Me Thy Heart" from the Book of Proverbs. The message spoke directly to my heart, mind, and soul. It found me exactly where I was and had been. "The Sword of the Word" cut left and right, and I could feel the pain and wounds from the sword. It was cutting away the desire for sin, and the weights began to fall off. However, I could also feel the medicine and oil from the Holy Ghost being poured in, healing, healing, smoothing and soothing every area of me! It was almost like a mother who soothes and strokes her crying baby, reassuring the baby of her nearness, love, and safety!

Those that were with me had to practically carry me through the streets of New York to where we were staying because I was so intoxicated by the Word of God and the freedom that I felt. I remember lying on the bed unable to sleep, crying all night long and releasing all those years and years of pain, hurts, and pent–up emotions. When day dawned, there was a new dawning not only in my soul, but all over me! I knew that the healing process had begun (I did not say completed). I now had strength to say no to satan and sin. Not that this strength had not been given to me at salvation, but I did not have the knowledge of the fullness of God's power, nor did I know how to appropriate this power.

Yes, I had read it, but it was not heart knowledge. Mostly, it was shouting, feeling good, do this and don't do that. Never direct teachings on specific issues. If an issue was brought up, it was addressed with such sternness and harshness, never with love. As I look back at it now, I realize that those who were instructing us did it the only way they knew and how they were reared. I also began to realize that my mother could only give me what she had. That realization helped me to finally forgive my mother.

I had allowed the circumstances of my life to bury the little knowledge that I did have so deep that it could not be activated and released because of layers and layers of garbage. When I came to myself, I began to realize that God had not failed me nor hurt me, only man. He had not done anything to me. It was I who walked away from God; it was I who decided that I would not forgive nor forget. It was I who decided that I would get even, not realizing that I would become entrapped by this desire. I had constantly justified my feelings over and over again because I was so young when the pain was inflicted on me. This justifying was now swept away; the excuses were swept away by the Spirit of God through His Word. The restoration process had now begun. Praise God!!!

Now, I had to accept the responsibility of having my life changed from this sick, dilapidated, angry, obnoxious person to the person that God intended me to be, and that person that I always wanted to be before my dream was shattered. I had to allow God to operate on my heart; I had to learn to love again; I had to learn to love myself and walk out of guilt and fear, and forgive those that injured me; but above all, I had to walk out of, resist, and forsake sin. I had to hate sin and its originator, satan. I also had to repent and acknowledge my disobedience. Oh, the mercy of God!! Even when we mess up God is still a God of chances. Don't let this moment pass you by!

You too must accept the responsibility for change. The ball is in your court. You cannot afford to be comfortable in your situation. You alone must be willing to acknowledge that there must be, it is imperative, expedient, and urgent that there be a cleaning out of the inner man, a flushing out of bitterness, anger, and unforgiveness. It must be dug out at the root and destroyed by the Power of God and yourself. You must open your hand, your clenched fist, and release the thing that has hurt you so deeply. You must relinquish your will.

Thomas Hasting and Augusta Toplady so fitly expressed this as they were inspired by God to pen the hymn "Rock of Ages". They wrote in the third stanza:

"Nothing in my hands I bring, Simply to the cross I cling; Naked, come to Thee for dress; Helpless look to Thee for grace; Foul, I to the fountain fly, Wash me, Savior, or I die."

We cannot bargain with God because we have nothing in our hands fit to bargain with, nor can He be bribed to take a short cut. We must cooperate with and surrender to the Holy Spirit in this intensive surgery in order to cut out this cancerous, foul disease before it consumes you. This operation is painful, but expedient — there is no time to procrastinate. **You must not die!**

In Heb. 4:13–16, I hear the Lord saying to me: "Yes, my people can come boldly to the throne of grace to find help in the time of need, but often when they come before me in the throne room, I will certainly prescribe what they need to help them. More often than not, it is intense emergency surgery because a new heart and the right spirit is that which is desperately needed!" In the Potter's House there is a surgical suite located behind the throne room. Therefore, don't kick and fight, just yield to the hands of the Master Surgeon. He will not grab us and throw us up on the operating table; we must be willing, with His directions along with His assistants (the host of angels), to get up on the table, and submit to the hand of the Master Surgeon as David did in (Ps. 51). How sweet it was when I stopped fighting and yielded to the hand of the Master. He began the surgery that only He knows how to perform! I was on my way out... I mean Out!!!

Did you come for help? Yes, you might say that your feelings were justified, as I did because you did not ask for this, but we must come out of our hiding place, forget the reasoning, get up on that table, and be willing to let God expose the places of infection and dig out or cut away the rotten, stinking flesh. Remove the fence of privacy; do not pull the cover up on yourself, for you need not be ashamed before The Healer because He saw your nakedness before you saw it. Stop being concerned about what people will say or what they think. <u>There are warts on your soul!</u>

Yes, there will be many lonely days and nights as you remain in intensive care under the wings and shadow of the Most High God. You will be separated from family and friends because the great physician will give orders that no visitors are allowed in order to keep you safe from outside contamination. You are being isolated by Dr. Jesus, Himself. This severe operation has been performed: a new heart, a new mind, a new spirit, and a new desire have replaced the old ones, but you are not yet ready to leave ICU. You must remain under watchful eyes and receive all treatments in order to insure full recovery. The diagnosis was "Death Impending: but, praise be to God, the prognosis is now "Full Recovery at Rapid Speed."

No, family and friends will not understand and will say that you are acting strange and that your doctor had no right to give such orders, "after all, we are family or I am your best buddy." Well, they thought you were acting strange anyway. They could not help you before, nor did some of them want to because they left you dying on the Jericho Road! Furthermore, it will not matter what they have to say because you really do not want to talk to anyone yet, nor do you wish to be pounced upon by curiosity seekers... you are in recovery.

Jesus will bind up your broken heart and spirit. He is the health of your countenance, and He will give you liberty from your imprisonment. He will break the bands and open the prison doors.

All that He asks you to do is to put on your sandals; it is time to move, to walk out of your dilemma. Make haste and get out, even as the angel commanded Peter to do in Acts 12:5–11. For even in prison, the light of God will shine to show you the way out. How wonderful it is to be freed from the dungeon of sin, hatred, unforgiveness, bitterness, confusion, all those crazy things that were jumping around in your head in the pigs' pen. It is simply marvelous!!!!

As you open your mouth and confess it, tell it, and expose it, which is called repentance and testimony, that demonic spirit of fear which brought you such torment, anger, unforgiveness, hatred, jealousy, emulation, wrath (the desire to get even), rejection, and bitterness will be exposed and satan's hiding places, those strongholds, will be brought to light and torn down — satan will no longer be able to blackmail you. How well I learned this lesson; this is why I openly tell my own story! I am free from satan's clutches.

Yes, there is a fight involved in the process of pulling down the strongholds, for we are breaking agreement with the foe who will fight to remain in our life. Demonic spirits cannot stand the light of God, who is the Word, the discerner of every thought and intent of the heart (Heb. 4:12). The Word of God is quicker and powerful and sharper than any two edged sword. Yes, satan will put up a fight to remain and not give up his territory, but if you will let EL ELYON, THE STRONGEST STRONG ONE, JESUS, coming in and completely occupy every area, every corner and every crevice of the house (you), satan and all of his demons must take up their wares and flee.

After all, Jesus did triumph over satan, and did take from satan the keys to death and hell. Therefore, The Sprit of the Lord will lift up a standard against him. You will then have greater power to keep him out of your house as you begin to experience freedom from these oppressive spirits. You will refuse to let them take up an abode in your house again, for the Strongest Strong one, Jesus, now answers the door, not you. EL ELYON NOW ANSWERS THE DOOR OF MY HOUSE: The Holy Ghost has made my body, mind, and soul fit for the Master to dwell in. He is Lord on the throne of my heart, mind, body, and soul... thank you Lord! To God be the glory for the great things He has done and is doing!!!

The double—minded person who once was is now dead (the one who only knew how to serve God with my head and not my heart), that person, the old me, has been crucified by the love and blood of Jesus Christ. I had to give up my ways and thoughts and take on the mind of God who said, "Be ye holy, for I am holy." I had to sanctify and set myself apart from my past life, so that God could become Lord of my life (Lev. 20:7—8; 1Pet. 1:15—19).

As I became obedient to the things of God and relinquished my entire self to Him, my life became prosperous, peaceful, and I was reassured of whom I am in Christ Jesus, who is my all in all. I am no longer afraid, or intimidated by anything or anyone. The pigs' pen experience was good for me in a sense. It taught me that the arms of flesh will fail you. It also taught me how to humble myself and how not to condemn, but to have mercy and love for others as God loved me and extended His mercy to me. It has also taught me how people can change no matter how low they find themselves. I NOW KNOW WHO I AM AND I CAN WALK TALL. WOW, IT IS NOW SO WONDERFUL!!!!!!

Delores Russ

TRUTH AND FREEDOM

Truth is often hard to deal with because there is a price attached to truth in order to obtain freedom. The price is that you must acknowledge and admit that there is something wrong, and you must go for help. In spite of all opposition from friends and church members, you can no longer be afraid of what they will say or what they won't say because the kingdom of satan has taken control of your life. Truth helps you to look squarely at yourself without pretense. It breaks down your wall and self will. It exposes the person that you have become as a result of the injury to your being. In fact, truth bares you, making you naked before God, but afterward, it will clothe you in righteousness.

Truth allows you to say, "I know I need help"; I know it because I feel it; I eat with it; I sleep with it, and I awake with it! Sometimes I speak with courage before others, but when I am alone there is this gut feeling of total defeat corroding away the inner being. Yes, you have tried to ignore it and pretend that it does not exist, but you are stuck and the residue has almost wrapped itself around every organ within you. It did not just begin; it has and is causing deformities. Your mind is under attack, you are fearful, almost terrified. There is no balance in your life, spiritually or naturally. You have lost the little bit of courage and confidence that you did have because the deep–seated spirit of anger and bitterness has been fertilized by unforgiveness. Its roots are spreading all through your body, mind, soul, and spirit. It is consuming you; it has become a tree; In fact, satan has hung his ornaments (the works of the flesh) on the branches of the tree.

Truth will liberate and set you free from the stronghold of satan, from the slavery of the past, people's opinions, fears, broken dreams, and even yourself. You must get to the only source of your complete freedom. **I say to you, I Plead With You! You Must Get Free and Remain Free! It Is Imperative or You will Die! You must not self destruct!!**

Who and what is this freedom? This freedom is the sphere of truth and life which is God Himself. This truth, freedom and life was presented to the world is in the person of Jesus Christ (Jn. 14:6; I Jn 5:6–12), who has passed into the heavens and is now our High Priest, who is always making intercessions for us before the Father. Therefore, He can be touched with the feelings of our infirmities, because He see us and knows our every need (He. 4:13–16).

Only God can deal with who we were, who we are, who we are not, and who we can become. Only Jesus can remove the rocks and break up the fallow ground, which is good ground that has become hard and stony because it has been left untilled for so long. Therefore, only God can cultivate the land, and cause it to produce fruit, the kind of fruit that will remain. Only He can make the heart pliable and tender again.

Many are turning to sexual explorations of all kinds, various medications, sleeping pills, hypnosis, transcendental meditation, psychics, tarot cards, horoscopes, tea—leaf reading, fortune tellers, and all other kinds of demonic activities trying to find the cure; But, these things definitely cannot give the answer because the one who is causing the depression, unforgiveness, anger, near nervous breakdowns, and the desire to get even is in control of these things, and that one is satan and his kingdom. So how in the world can these activities which he controls help us. He is not about to let you go free.

The Psychologist, the Psychiatrist, and the Christian Counselor are wonderful people, and we thank God for them, but they cannot really get to the root cause and bring total, complete healing in ones life. Only Jesus can do this!!! Only Jesus can give you the answer, for He is the answer.

Let me give you two examples of those who received healing and deliverance by the power of God because they were placed in an area of truth which led to their freedom.

**On one occasion, I was ministering in another state at a morning session for women who were single, separated, divorced, and widowed. As I sat in that room crowded full of women who wanted an answer for their dilemma, in walked this stunning, beautiful sister whose presence filled the room. Immediately, the Lord spoke to me and told me to call her up front and sit her at my table, and He would show me what her needs were. She did not know that she had come for her inner healing that day. When I asked that she come to the front table, she insisted that she wanted to sit at the back table (a good hiding place). Of course, I insisted by the authority of the Holy Spirit that she move up front which she eventually did out of obedience.

As I sat quietly before ministering, the Holy Ghost began to boomerang in my head. He began to reveal to me areas in this sister's life that had kept her imprisoned for years and that needed to be healed desperately. **It is so wonderful to know that the Spirit of God does reveal the deep and hidden things as His Spirit intercepts with our spirit because only the Spirit knows what is in us (Rm. 8:27; I Co. 2:11). He indeed does know us altogether!!!**

As I began to teach, exhort and share some of my own testimony, this same sister jumped up and began to scream, holler, cry, and stomp the floor. She ran forward, grabbed me around my neck, fell on my shoulders, and began sobbing, mourning, and groaning very deeply. Over and over again she sobbed and cried, "help me, help me, help me." Her weight was so much that it almost pushed me to the floor. I nodded for someone to get me a chair, and I was assisted in sitting down with this sister still clinging around my neck. She sat in my lap like a tiny child, literally balled up with her knees in my chest and stomach, sobbing and sobbing until she was spent.

As I sat in that position for about 10 minutes, the Lord began to reveal to me that this dear beloved sister had been a victim of incest and rape which had happened to her numerous times. After she was able to talk, she confirmed that she had indeed been a victim of rape and incest at an early age by her brother and uncle. She was never able to rid herself of the shame and guilt. She always felt dirty and betrayed. She had been through two marriages, but both ended in disaster. Yes, she was a very beautiful, attractive woman, held a top executive job in this city and drove a luxurious car, but those things did not answer the needs or give her a way out of her prison, nor did they liberate her or bring freedom because she was so very broken inside from past injuries to her person.

This beloved sister had never been able to tell her story, except to her mother who dared her to reveal the truth. She did not trust anyone with this hidden area of her life. But, that morning the Holy Sprit opened up those dark places in order that she could walk into her freedom. As we continued to minister to her in privacy with much love, tenderness, and compassion, yet with all spiritual authority, God began the cleansing and healing process. We witnessed a transformation from the old to the new, a walk out of prison into freedom and into the light of God; The chains fell off!

Since that time, she has called to share another and another of those inner secrets and concerns, or if fear tries to over take her. I always attempt to speak to her the Words of Spirit and Life which are the continuing sunshine for our soul. I also share with her the overcoming victories that God has helped me to obtain. The calls are not nearly as frequent as before because each time I see her, she has reached another level of maturity which has ensured her continued freedom. JESUS DOES SET THE CAPTIVE FREE!!

**On another occasion, I was ministering at a retreat, and I broke the attendees down into small groups to discuss a case study the Lord had given me to write. As we adventured into this particular case study pertaining to a marriage that was about to collapse, this one sister began to give her opinion on the study, but stated that her marriage was a very happy, solid marriage. At the end of the group session, this same sister gave the summarization for her group, and continued to maintain that her marriage was very happy and that she could only relate to the case study in a small way. However, at the time of personal ministering, I was led to embrace this sister because the Lord, through His Spirit, allowed me to hear something else. As I took her in my arms and held her very close, she began to cry violently. I continued to hold her until she stopped crying. She admitted that her marriage was in chaos and almost totally disintegrated because of fear, and she was controlled by her mother who was a witchcraft worker.

As we, myself, and other ministers who were anointed in deliverance ministry, began to address the spirit of witchcraft, control, manipulation and fear, this sister began to vomit. She vomited all over the sleeve of my blouse, on my skirt, and on the floor. She regurgitated over and over. I thank God for those who came with me to assist me in ministering because they were able to act quickly in cleaning me up, the floor and the sister, in order that I would not be distracted in the delivery process.

As those spirits were addressed, this sister fell out in the floor, her eyes rolled back in her head and the spirits began to speak out of her. She then went into a state of unconsciousness. By the might power of the Holy Ghost, we had to cast out not only that spirit of fear and control, but numerous other demons that accompanied the two main spirits. We refused to stop until the Lord let us know that our work was finished. At that point the sister came back to herself and began to cry like a little child. The real her surfaced which had never been allowed to grow up because of the control of her mother. This was truly her season to walk out of fear and the control of witchcraft. The Spirit of God knows how to orchestrate the setting of truth, and bring us freedom from our places of bondage and imprisonment! It never ceases to amaze me at what God does. This is why we cannot take credit for anything... it's God all the way!!

By permission of this sister, I consulted with her pastor who was more than willing to provide the after—care because she could not be left without this much needed follow—up. After almost one year, she and her husband reconciled and moved to another state. She is still under the watchful eyes of a very excellent, Spirit—filled pastor. It is so very important that the house not only be swept and garnished, but it must be occupied by **The Strongest Strong man, El Elyon, Jesus Christ who is well able to guard and protect what belongs to Him.**

Jesus is the absolute pardon of our debt, He is our bail. We are forever acquitted, exonerated and discharged. The document is sealed; the content is not remembered any more. God does not condemn us, but He restores us . . . Totally!!!! "If we confess our sins, He is faithful and just to forgive us our sins, and cleanse us from all unrighteousness" (I John 1:9). We will not only be forgiven, but healed and preferred, holy priest, even as Joshua the high priest in Zechariah 3:1—5. "The filthy garments will be taken away, your iniquity will pass away, you will be clothed with new garments, and a fair miter will be placed upon your head."

I know that this account of Joshua is a type of the restoration of the church, but I and you are a part of the church; therefore, we are included in the restoration. Again, God does not condemn us, but justifies and restores us, Praise God. We should be encouraged by the Word of God in Romans 8:33—34 (Amplified Bible):

"Who can bring any charge against God's elect (when it is) God who justifies — Who put us in right relation to Himself? (Who shall come forward and accuse or impeach those whom God has chosen? Will God, Who acquits us?) Who is there to condemn (us)? Will Christ Jesus, the Messiah, who died, or rather who was raised from the dead, who is at the right hand of God actually pleading as He intercedes for us?"

JESUS IS OUR HIGH PRIEST, PRAISE GOD AND AMEN!!!

The Truth of God is often painful because it has a way of "getting into our business, and it speaks directly to our mess, but if we will embrace God's truth, we will find the path to freedom, liberty and abundant living. The truth is bitter, but sweet. As we maintain a regular diet of truth, we will begin to experience the rest and peace of God.

God's truth brings wisdom and understanding to live by on a daily basis. Proverbs 3:13 lets us know that we are happy when we find wisdom and get understanding. Embrace and hold God's truth as precious jewelry. It is so costly and of great price which cannot be calculated. Hold it dear to your heart.

HE RESTORETH MY SOUL

The scripture plainly shows us that when the Prodigal son returned home to his father, the father did not ask a lot of questions like we do, but loved him and welcomed him home. The father restored him to his rightful position by putting on him the best robe, a ring on his finger and shoes on his feet. Though the son had spent all of his own inheritance, the father had enough love, mercy, and wealth to give his son more out of his abundant riches. Our Father is the same. For He will: "Restore unto you all the years that the locust has eaten, the cankerworm, the caterpillar, and the palmerworm, my great army which I sent among you. And you shall eat in plenty, and be satisfied, and praise the name of the Lord your God, that has dealt wondrously with you: and My people shall never be ashamed" (Joel 2:25–26).

I can say that I have more now than I did 52 years ago, both spiritually and naturally. God has restored unto me an abundance out of His treasure that is never depleted. Even if God gives every person on this earth out of His treasure, it will never run out... He is The I Am, That I Am. Praise His Wonderful Name!

The Father, God, liberates us by His wonderful, sweet, eternal mercy and love, which helps and assists us in our spiritual growth. Therefore, only in the climate of liberty and restoration can love grow because in this climate, the ground is fertile and has the ability to produce great abundance of fruit which will remain.

Kingdom women (and men) must be present in every moment of life, for Jesus said, "I am come that you might have life and that more abundantly (Jn. 10:10) ——I've come to restore your soul. Once the soul is restored, the rest of us will come into compliance with the law of liberty, and we will begin to abound more and more.

You must feel life, enjoy life, ever learning, ever exploring, and ever appreciating the world God made and the people in it, **but above all, loving and appreciating yourself.** You must stop blaming yourself or the circumstances for your near demise, but live. Once you begin to realize that life is still worth reaching for, and you must and can go on no matter what has happened in your life (rape, incest, abusive parents, sexual molestation, broken marriage, betrayal, etc.), you will begin to live and not die, to declare the works of the Lord (Ps. 118:17). Someone else needs to know the work that God has wrought in your life!

The peace, happiness, joy, victory and the pulse beat of life which you have searched for is within you, rather than outside of you. The kingdom of God is within you and there is peace, love, and joy in the Holy Spirit. Life is too big, beautiful, and full of meaning to stop at one junction.

In finding God's freedom, the hurt will no longer choke the life out of you. There will be a new infusion of love, life, and liberty – a new beginning. You will begin to love yourself, even if the childhood dreams were not fulfilled. There are still other dreams and goals for which to reach! You will forgive the one who injured you so deeply because if we want Christ's forgiveness, we must forgive those who trespassed against us. But above and foremost, you will forgive yourself. You will lose the desire for hate and all of its components. Forgiveness is not an option, but a vital necessity!

I will never forget the night that I knelt beside my children's bed and asked God to take away the hate and the frantic desire to get even with my mate, my mother, and those who had hurt me so deeply. Jesus answered my prayers. Even now, the memory is still there, but the pain and evil desires have gone. No longer does it haunt me, nor do I cry about what was. What was is now my testimony to others of what God can do in one's life. It is my testimony how God can transform us and make us new through His Son Jesus Christ. The life which I now live in the flesh, I live by faith of the Son of God, who loves me and gave Himself for me (Ga. 2:20(b).

In forgiveness there is freedom! You begin to understand the destiny of your life. You no longer wallow in hurt, loneliness, unforgiveness, and endless hopelessness. The waste matter will be recycled and turned into positive energy. You will take the same experience that you were delivered from and help others to be healed who are like you were. The very thing that was meant for evil to destroy you has now been turned to good, giving you a deeper understanding of others and helping to activate the ministry of reconciliation in your life. No longer do you sit in judgment or condemnation, but in mercy, love, healing, and helping to restore others.

As I said before, it is very hard to understand why God would allow certain things to happen in our lives, but it will work for our good, and the good of the kingdom of God if we do not allow it to entrap us forever. Even if it does entrap us temporarily, there is a Rescuer, Jesus who will deliver us from all distress if we "come clean" with Him. Therefore, those things must not be a stopping point, but a launching pad of healing wherein we can soar to greater heights as a women of God. I thank God that I found this freedom and liberty through the power of God!

You are God's elect and you will become a woman of stability, sturdy, easily entreated, unmoveable, full of compassion and love. You are a woman who will weather the future storms without panic (yes, there are some more), and will help others to weather their storms. The Apostle Paul states in Phil. 3:13–14 (KJV):

> Brethren, I count not myself to have apprehended: but this one thing I do, forgetting those things which are behind, and reaching forth unto those things which are before. I press (steadily pushing, thrusting while in contact, constrain, force, exert pressure; push ones way toward, aim, direct ones course; progressive) toward the mark for the prize of the high calling of God in Christ Jesus.

You will forget those things which were behind and reach for the newness or the renewal of your life. By the power of God and your cooperation, you can openly confront the issues. No longer are they swept under the rug, hid in the closet, or non–discussable issues. I believe Paul dealt with all of his past issues on the backside of the

Arabian desert; this is why he could say, "I forget those things which are behind, and I reach for those things which are before."

No, some things are not easily forgotten in the natural realm, but in the realm of the Spirit the pain ceases and the mind becomes refocused. The Holy Spirit is our Enabler. No longer will you spend sleepless nights and every awakening moment agonizing over and rehearsing what was or what could have been, nor what and who it was that hurt you and shattered your dreams — It is so wonderful.

You will now push and exert pressure toward living. Anything or anyone that tries to stop you or get in your way is in danger of being run over. You will come out fighting, and nothing will send you back into that prison. Anyone who has tasted of freedom will settle for nothing less. You do not just want to survive, but live!! Yes, you want to live in wholeness, that abundant life. One can survive on bread and water, but God wants us to live and have some of the "caviar and filet mignon" of life.

You must put all of your emotions, your entire life and the keeping of your soul into God's hands. You must continually renew the spirit of your mind and discipline your thoughts. For what one feeds the mind is what will nurture the mind's actions, and in turn the spirit man and the body. What you put in is what you get out (Phil. 4:8) (II Co. 10:5–7). Speak to yourself, fight the good fight of faith, and stay away from negative people, even if they are your friends. You do not need friends or associates who never have anything good to say, gossipers, and those who are full of criticism, gloomy, contrary, and down right cantankerous. It might seem strange to be without these type of people for a while, but you will begin to feel 75 pounds lighter.

Two still cannot walk together except they agree. You must never again agree with anyone who will try to make you negative again. You do not have to be rude to people, but you do not need a lot of outside advice. Your ears are now attuned to Jesus, and you are now seeking the kingdom and all His righteousness; therefore, God knows whom to direct you to if He feels earthly assistance is needed.

Believe me, God does have those in the flesh who are spiritual midwives who are ready to assist you without trying to claim you as their own. They realize that you belong to God and God alone. Be careful how you let people take credit for your deliverance. It was God who did it, not the preacher, the teacher, your mother, your father, the bishop or "mother–so–and–so." Yes, we give honor to these people, but they were only the instruments used by God if they had any part in the process at all. Therefore, we give all the glory and adoration to God and God alone.

Though the complete healing process does not happen over night, hold onto your faith knowing that, "He who has begun a good work in you will perform it until the day of Jesus of Christ." (Phil. 1:6). Because each person is different, the healing process is quicker for some and longer for others, but it will happen. It will happen as soon as you allow it to, by deciding that you will not fight, kick, scream, and holler. As in childbirth, the longer you scream, kick, holler, and do not move with the pain by pushing and bearing down, the longer the labor.

Once you cooperate in the birthing process, the pain and the hurt will reach its final climax. After it is over, you will then stand tall; no longer will your back be bent or your shoulders rounded because of the heavy load. You will have a new attitude and a new testimony.

You will be strengthened with might in the inner man and outer man. No, the fight does not cease because the "old–man" which is controlled by our flesh, always tries to get us to resurrect it again; But you must know that you have the very God of glory living in you, "the treasure in earthen vessel", and you must "Likewise, reckon ye also yourselves to be dead indeed unto sin, but alive unto God through Jesus Christ Our Lord" (Ro. 6:11).

You must also realize that you are no match for the devil, but your God Is! Jesus is the one who got the keys of death and hell. It was He who triumphed over demonic powers to obtain and secure victory for His "Called Out Ones." It was He who set the captive free. It is He who gives us the Power of His Spirit in order to resist the power, the control and the influence of satan and his kingdom. God is invincible and so are we if we abide in Him, and He in us; Therefore, we cannot be defeated, destroyed or overthrown (II Co. 4:6–9).

God will fortify you for life and true living in the Kingdom of God. There will be contentment, peace, and confidence. Yes, restlessness will sometimes try to set in, but you will find that solitary place with God where you will again be strengthened for your next level of maturity. No longer will you desire to return to that place of your near demise – Praise God.

Remember, Peter, who when he saw Jesus walking on the water, asked Jesus to let him get out of the boat and walk on the water also. Well, Jesus bid him to come, and he did began to walk on the water for a short time; However, when he saw the wind become turbulent and boisterous, Peter became afraid and began to sink. Thank God Peter knew what to do, he cried out, "Lord save me." Immediately Jesus stretched forth his hand and caught him (Mt. 14:28–31). The winds of the past will blow trying to cause you to become afraid and sink. Don't look at the winds, but look at Jesus. Even if you do look at the wind, never ever be afraid to call out to God for help. He will catch you. He will not let you sink, nor will He let the waters overflow you (Is. 43:1.2). God Is In Control, Amen.

Jesus promised never to leave us nor forsake us, and He is true to His promise. What He says is yea and amen. We can join with David in Ps. 23:4: "Yea though I walk through the valley and shadow of death, I will fear no evil: for Thy art with me: Thy rod and Thy staff they comfort me." David did not say that he was going to the valley to stay, but that he was only walking through the valley because there was a lesson to be learned in the valley. He was confident that his God would bring him out, and in the process restore his soul. We must also be confident that the valley nor death can hold us because Jesus conquered death, and He is the lily of the valley.

When your soul is truly restored (Ps. 23:3), you will go anywhere God leads whether it is on the mountain or valley, in the hills or plains, for He is walking ahead, leading the sheep with Heavenly Rerewarders behind. You will come out victoriously as Jesus did in His wilderness experience (Matt. 4:1–11). You can do all things through Christ who strengthen you (Phil.4:13).

God wants us restored because He desires:

1. That we be whole both spirit, soul, and body.
2. That we be honorable vessels fit for His use.
3. That the place of His abode be free from sickness, germs and debris.

4. That our bodies be full of light and become transmitters of that light, generating power and spiritual energy, dispersing darkness in order that souls will be won to Him.

5. That we come into our fullest potentials as sons of God, with the character and likeness of Jesus.

6. That we be filled with the knowledge of His will, in all wisdom and spiritual understanding (Col. 3:9).

7. That our ground be fertile producing good, wholesome fruit which will minister to the hungry.

Jesus paid an awful, awesome and terrible price for our redemption. He bought us back from the clutches of sin with His own blood in order to reclaim us as His own; therefore, God will do whatever is necessary to let satan and all the host of hell know that we are His property. We are no longer our own, but His. We have been bought with a price that far exceeds and is more costly than diamonds, silver, gold or the rarest stones, or anything else that money can buy. Yes, we have been purchased with the precious blood of Jesus, who was willing to shed His blood, and give up His life for you and me. He did it all because He so loved us even when we were His enemies – what love!

Jesus, who was born of a woman did crush the head of satan as promised (Gen. 3:15). Since Jesus was the first born (seed) among many brethren, there are some more righteous seed that must be brought forth to continue to crush satan's head. This is why satan seeks to destroy women who receive and carry the seed, future sons of God (sons do not denote any gender).

Stay under the mighty hands of God for restoration, so you can be made fit to carry forth your divine purpose and destiny in God, a woman fit for the master's use. Remember, nothing is impossible with God, and there is nothing too difficult for Him. He is the God of all flesh!

THE WITNESSES

The Bible records in the book of Genesis, chapters 37–50, the account of Joseph, the son of Jacob. Joseph was a dreamer who dreamed dreams which he shared with his brothers. They disliked Joseph because their father Jacob loved Joseph more than any of his other sons, since Joseph was the son of his old age. (Gen. 37:30)

After telling his brothers his dreams, which predicted that Joseph would reign over them, they plotted against Joseph to kill him, but his brother Reuben stopped his brothers from doing so. Instead, they cast him into a pit and eventually sold him for twenty pieces of silver to a company of Ishmelites who carried Joseph to Egypt. There in Egypt, Joseph found favor with Potiphar, the captain of the guards of Pharaoh's army.

Even in the house of Potiphar the enemy plotted against Joseph which caused him to be cast into prison because of false accusations from Potiphar's wife, who seemingly had the evidence in her hands (Joseph's garment) to prove or verify that he was guilty, but God was with Joseph. Even in these adverse circumstances, God had greater plans for Joseph, not just to oversee one man's house, but to govern nations.

It was the "God given ability" of Joseph that enabled him to interpret the dreams of the chief butler and the chief baker who were imprisoned with Joseph, and who eventually helped secure Joseph's release. The chief butler forgot about Joseph after being restored to Pharaoh's service just as Joseph had predicted. The baker was hung just as Joseph had also predicted; but again, God had not forgotten Joseph.

After two (2) years of being imprisoned, God caused Pharaoh to have a dream and the king sent for Joseph, per the recommendations of the chief butler who serves the king and was the closest one to him. Joseph interpreted the dream of Pharaoh exactly and precisely, predicting what would happen in Egypt for the next 14 years. How marvelous God is! He knows all things and sees all things. He knows the beginning from the end, and He will reveal great and might things to His servants.

As a result of his ability and fore–knowledge, Joseph was made ruler over all that Pharaoh had because Pharaoh recognized that the Spirit of God dwelled in the dreamer, Joseph. Thus was the beginning of the fulfillment of the dreams that Joseph had in his youth, but also the beginning of the prophecy that God gave to Abram in Genesis 15:13–14.

Joseph not only fed this great nation of Egypt and surrounding areas for over 14 years in famine, but he also fed, reconciled, and restored his own family who thought that he was dead. But above and beyond all, Joseph forgave his brothers who tried to kill him. Joseph prospered because God had a plan for his life and the nation of Israel. Joseph held on to his God and his integrity.

Yes, the enemy has tried to destroy you along with your dream, but if the dream is from God in due time it shall come to pass. He will give you much better and more abundantly than you can ever imagine. What He gives will certainly supersede and is certainly superior to anything that you went out on our own to get, or anything you try to accomplish on your own.

Job suffered great loss, but when that period of suffering ended, Job had more at the end than he had at the beginning (Job 42:10–16). Not only did God give him new sons and daughters, but God also gave him greater wealth.

Job's blessings and renewed prosperity came only after he had a direct face to face encounter with God. Once he realized that he not only heard God with his ears, but had seen Him with his eyes, then was Job able to forgive and pray for his friends who had accused him of evil and wrong doings. They said that Job deserved what came upon him (as many has said about us). Also, Job had to acknowledge and repent for speaking bitterly about the thing that had happened to him because Job had actually spoken against God. The blessings of repentance and forgiveness are restoration and clarity.

Job had an experience that no one could take from him. He had a story to tell others. Not what he heard, but what he knew for himself – so shall you. The account is not left on record for us to merely shout over, but as an example of what God can and will do for us. You too have a testimony that you alone know and can tell. Not something that someone else told you, but first hand experience. Just as the Samaritans said unto the Samaritan Woman after going to see

Jesus whom this woman had told them about: "Now we believe, not because of the saying for we have heard Him ourselves, and know that this is indeed the Christ, the Savior of the world." (John 4:42)

If you wait on the Lord, whatsoever God has for you shall come to pass, for what He said, He shall perform it. The dark is just before the dawn, the sowing before the reaping, and the blessings after the healing. The seed must first fall into the ground and die, then the springing forth of new life, and then the harvest. You will look back and marvel at the reaping, because you felt that nothing could ever be produced from your ground that was so hard and unyielding. Thanks be to God for the fertilizing of the ground with love and mercy. The Holy Spirit removes all stones and stubble, and cultivates the ground to receive the good seed.

Paul so beautifully gives hope and insight into the One who brings about healing, the process and the final results, which make us productive people of God:

> I have planted, Apollos watereth: but God gave the increase. So then neither is he that planteth anything, neither he that watereth; but God that giveth the increase. (I Co. 3:6–7)

God desires to prosper His people with increase. Prosperity is not always in dollars and cents, for what good is material wealth without peace, happiness, joy, hope, love, trust and contentment. If one is broken and crippled inside, almost near dead, nothing really matters anyway, not even the millions of dollars one may acquire. The Lord desires that we prosper in health(body), but foremost and above all is that our souls prosper. "What shall it profit a man if he shall gain the whole world, and lose his own soul (Mk. 8:36)? But seek ye first the kingdom of God and His righteousness; and all these things shall be added unto you" (Mt. 6:33).

We read the Bible and constantly testify and rejoice about the testimonies of the various Bible personalities, but I am convinced that God wants us to have our own testimonies. Our testimonies coming out of experience (whether good or bad) are our most powerful weapons against the devil.

The Word of God declares in Revelations 12:11:

> "And they overcame him by the blood of the Lamb, and by the word of their testimony; and they loved not their lives unto the death."

We can truly rejoice when we look back and know that it was God who brought us up and out. We can be true witnesses of the God who is the same yesterday, today, and shall forever be. Jesus is our health, strength and the lifter up of our head. There is hope because the hurts and wounds shall be completely healed to the core, and all infections stopped! **Brand new skin will come over a brand new person! We are a victorious people!!**

Many of you want to marry for the first time, or remarry again, while others desire to remain single. God knows and you know that you are not ready nor prepared for life and living no matter what status you choose until you rid yourself of the past. You cannot go on to the future with or without a mate until the hurt is healed. You can only find healing as you recess into the presence of God, who is the Author and Finisher of our faith. He is the only true foundation upon which you can build the future. Make certain that all of your choices are in God's will; if not, you will be right back in the pig's-pen.

If you build your house upon the sand it will fall, but if you build your house upon the rock, the sure foundation which is Jesus, who is love, faith, peace, truth, and trustworthy, it will stand throughout eternity. You must know and believe that Jesus can and does heal the broken hearted. He does heal the hurt and restore the soul right in the presence of those who thought that you were going down for the last time, but before the last count (the twelve o'clock hour), the hands that were hung down were lifted, and the feeble knees given strength (Hebrews 12:12–13).

You will be a marvel to those who look upon you, and you will be a marvelous miracle to yourself. The Chief Shepherd, the lover of your soul, your Abba–Father restored your soul and is now leading you in the path of righteousness. Not by constraint or force, but because you now have a new desire to follow. You are now a new creature, old things have passed away and all things are new. You are now walking and talking in the newness of God's life. No longer are you a cowering, fearful slave to satan's strongholds of what was, how it was, and who did it, because you are now walking in the sunlight of God's love. God does care for you and will cause you to triumph in Christ Jesus.

This will indeed be your testimony and witness with a great cloud of witnesses in heaven and on earth! We can indeed concur with the Psalmist David as he recorded in Ps. 30: 1–4, 8–12: (NKJV):

I will extol You, O Lord, for You have lifted me up, And have not let my foes rejoice over me. Lord My God, I cried out to You, and You <u>healed me</u>. Lord, You brought my soul from the grave; You have kept me alive. That I should not go down to the pit. I cried out to You, O Lord; and to the Lord I made supplication: "What profit is there in my blood, When I go down to the pit? Will the dust praise you? Will it declare Your truth? Hear, O Lord, and have mercy on me; Lord, be my helper!" You have turned for me my mourning into dancing; You have put off my sackcloth and clothed me with gladness, To the end that my glory may sing praise to you and not be silent. O Lord my God, I will give thanks to You forever.

CONCLUSION

The success to your continued healing and victory is so very important and will depend upon your moving in oneness with God!

There seems not to be enough hours in a day to accomplish all of the things that you have to do, but you **must make** the time to be alone with the Lord and yourself. You must pull back from everything for selected periods of time and find that place of solitude, the place where you shut out all other voices. You must find the place of quietness, the place of rest where you can be refreshed, reassured, and re—instructed. The more you do this, the more you will realize the necessity of doing so. In fact, you will enjoy doing so.

Take the telephone off the hook or unplug it, and take a day off from your job. If there are children, find a good support system that will assist you in caring for the children during this time of solitude. Remember, do not be overbearing or unwise in asking for assistance. If you are on a limited income save a few dollars and find a nice inexpensive retreat site for individual retreats, or find another quiet hideaway. Do not let too many people know where you are going except those who are necessary in case of an emergency.

During this time of solitude, release all of your concerns to God, and then sit in His presence quietly so that He can begin to remove the anxiety, give answers and then send the waters of refreshing into your being. There is peace in His presence; there is joy in His presence; there is love in His presence, and when you come out nothing else will matter. All of those things which seem to be insurmountable will be minute. Your walk will be different; your talk will be different and your vision will be clearer; in fact, the whole world and people will seem different.

It is also important to make time for quality prayer and meditation. Remember, you do not have to be in any particular position to pray; however, try to remove any distraction which would prevent you from giving yourself in total prayer, thanksgiving, and adoration to God. Things will come to your mind as you first begin your journey into the presence of God, but do not get weary or stop —— Stay there and persevere; wait quietly, and all hindering forces will flee. Before you know it, you will be enthroned in the presence of the Almighty God, your Father!

When Daniel prayed, the answer to his prayers were hindered until God dispatched angels to conquer the Prince of Persia, which represents satan, in order that Daniel could get clear instructions and understanding. Don't worry, God will come through for you and to you. Do not spend all the time talking; allow God to talk to you because God deals with the intent of the heart, and He loves to talk to us. There you can make known your request before God, and have sweet communion with your Savior, Friend, and The Beloved.

Ps. 16:11... "Thou will show me the path of life: in thy
presence there is fullness of joy; at thy right hand there
are pleasures for ever more."

Spiritual fasting is also very, very essential because it brings the
fleshly nature into submission to the Holy Spirit, causing your spirit
man to hear what the Spirit of God will speak. It is the fleshly, soulish
part of us that does not want to listen or obey (read II Co. 10:3–6).
There is something so tremendously fulfilling about fasting and prayer.
Fasting and prayer brings a stillness to you and your surroundings,
causing the fleshly thoughts to be harnessed and ceasing their control
(Romans 8:5,6 – Living Bible).

There has been much controversy and discussion about whether
we should fast unless we have been directed by God to do so. I believe
that Jesus has already directed us to do so in His statement to the
disciples when they could not cast the dumb and deaf spirit out of the
child, and they wanted to know why they could not: Jesus said, "this
kind can come forth by nothing, but prayer and fasting" (MK 9:29).
Fasting should never be done for an outside show, to impress others,
nor to present yourself as more holy than others (Mt. 6:16–18). This
is a special time given to your relationship with God, and especially
to deal with those dumb and deaf spirits that want to stay; but, they
definitely must leave God's habitation! This habitation, our body, was
fashioned for the Lord's presence, not dumb and deaf spirits that want
to prevent us from hearing the voice of God.

I have found both fasts, one that God calls or one that is chosen to
dedicate oneself unto the Lord to be highly beneficial and profitable.
There are times that the Lord directs me to fast, and then there are

times that I sanctify a time of intense fasting and prayer because I love the Lord and desire to be in His presence. So often there comes a deep restlessness and yearning to be in that special place with God. After all, He is not only my Savior and Lord, but also my lover and my best friend; Therefore, He does not always have to make the first move for us to be together, so I invite Him to sup with me. There I bow down and worship; there I give Him the fruit of my lips; there I bath in His glory and release all my concerns and find answers. I find rest near to the heart of God "praise His Name forever! Be certain to allow the Holy Spirit which lives inside of you to direct your path, not man's opinion.

My "Sisters do not always be so anxious to "hang—out" with the crowd or listen to their voices. We can be too busy doing church work and not attending to our soul or doing the work of the church, which extends beyond our local assemblies. In fact, the greatest work that we can do is in our homes and with ourselves. We must take inventory and assess what we are doing, who we are doing it for and where are we going? If what you are doing and where you are going is not for Jesus and His kingdom, it will never satisfy or keep you out of "the hole" that you were once in.

Philippians 4:8 states:

> "Finally, brethren, whatsoever things are true, whatsoever things are honest, whatsoever things are just, whatsoever things are pure, whatsoever things are lovely, whatsoever things are of a good report; if there be any virtue, and if there be any praise, think on these things.

I am convinced that there are many wonderful things in this world which are true, lovely, honest, and pure, but they have no virtue (moral excellence); therefore, they are not worth my thoughts nor do they bring praise to God. This does not mean that they have no meaning or usefulness to others, but they add nothing to my life as a son of God, nor do these things help me to excel in my walk with God.

I have learned, and so will you, that what is good for one person is not necessarily good for another. Always keep before you what and where God brought you from. You must not allow any impurities into your heart and spirit again. What someone else does or participates in, you cannot do. There are some things that you cannot handle or touch. Don't even look at it too long or allow it to penetrate your thought process. You must resist every attempt of satan to ensnare you again.

I had a very, dear, close friend, the late Evang. Dorothy Burnside, whom God so wonderfully saved, healed, and totally delivered from years of drug addiction and prostitution. What a mighty vessel for God was she! I remember her telling me a dream that she had about a school of fish. She said the water was so blue and beautiful in which the school of fish was swimming, but when she looked, there was one fish swimming alone by itself, never attempting to mingle with or catch—up with the other fish. When she awoke, she inquired of God what the dream meant. She said that the Lord told her that she was the one fish swimming alone; there was nothing wrong with what the other fish were doing, but because of what He had delivered her from, she could not swim with the other fish.

This woman of God could often be found moving by herself, not with the crowd. She set her standards high for God. My! What an anointed vessel of God who moved with great boldness, authority and power against the kingdom of darkness. She was endowed with the gift of discernment. She was highly respected and sought out for her godly wisdom because she dared to "be something different."

I learned from this that God does call us to be "a set aside vessel" for His glory, especially those who shall be called forth for special ministry. **It is indeed a challenge to be something different for God, even in the church world.** You must love people, be kind and friendly, but when God tells you to move away or step back, obey, obey, obey!! No, we will not be so different and strange that we can never associate with the members of the body of Christ or other persons, but when a summons comes from the Throne Room to appear and appear alone, not for punishment, but for revelation, knowledge, and new instruction, OBEY! Do not try to take anyone with you. In fact, do not even let others know of this time because they will try to infringe or tell you, "all this is not necessary!"

You must learn to channel your spiritual energies in the proper direction in order to have reserved energy for those times of need and crises, not necessarily your own needs or crises, but often those of others that God would have you minister to.

I am watching so many of God's women go from one conference to another, from one revival to another, searching for the excitement and thrill of the moment (how I know). <u>They scream, holler, jump and shake.</u> <u>They scream and holler some more</u>, but have no spiritual power to keep satan out of their lives (Oh, how I know), much less the lives of their families and others around them. Most do not even know what the preacher said. Some jot down notes if they can hear over the crowd or their own voices, and most times, these notes end up in a book or on a piece of paper until the next time, if there is a next time!

Remember, emotionalism does not mean that we are delivered, nor is it the keeping force of one's life. Satan is not impressed with our emotionalism, but the power of the Holy Spirit that is paramount in our lives. This Holy Ghost power is endowed upon us by God to enable us, to fortify us and to allow our mere presence to cause satanic powers to back up, even if we never open our mouths to speak. If we have to speak, the anointing of the Holy Sprit will so saturate our words that they will bring spirit and life to the listener. It is also essential to use your spiritual energies to prepare yourself for service and maturity as a son of God in the earth today. **Study the Word of God, allowing it to sink within your spirit man; rehearse the Word; memorize the Word, not just for head knowledge, but for heart transformation.** Love the Word, listen to the Word, and obey the Word. Many messages that we hear today or many words that God will put in our spirit man today will not be just for the today, but for the tomorrow.

You do not have to be a scholar to love and understand the Word of God. The scripture states in James 1:5 (NKJV): "If any of you lack wisdom, let him ask of God, who gives to all liberally, and without reproach, and it will be given him."

Paul states in Colossians 1:9–11:

> For this cause we also, since the day we heard it, do not cease to pray for you, and desire that you might

be filled with the knowledge of his will and spiritual understanding; That you might walk worthy of the Lord unto all pleasing, being fruitful in every good work, and increase in the knowledge of God; Strengthened with all might, according to his glorious power, unto all patience and longsuffering with joyfulness.

In order for the voice of God's Spirit to overtake all anxieties, frustrations and concerns and translate them into heavenly directions, it is an absolute necessity to allow the Word of God to still your spirit amidst such a noisy world. Without this translation, we will act and react according to the flesh causing us to make God ashamed, and again making ourselves ashamed. We must study and take time to discipline our mind and body to be quiet and still. Stillness is an art and power once learned will always be a part of making life very effective. Even when God is speaking some things that are not so pleasant or comfortable to the fleshly desires and wishes, they are still sweet to a matured son of God — Amen! Eventually, we will become excited about the correction of God because He chastens and corrects those whom He loves.

Allow God to order your steps by His Word. Each one of us is unique and special in the eyes of God, and He knows exactly what our daily diet should be... Please Follow the Plan for wholeness. It is the only way you will grow into a matured son of God in this present world, and be prepared to reign in that Eternal Place with The King of kings and The Lord of Lords — the Lamb Who sits on the throne. JESUS WAS THE LAMB THAT WAS SLAIN.

I and you must always keep in mind that God never wills sin of any kind, but the Mighty God, the Lamb upon the throne is the forgiver of sin. He will help us to clean up the mess through our repentance and acknowledgment that we need Him in every part of our life. He will take the mess and turn it into glory for His divine purpose. I am the woman that I am today because of God's love, His faithfulness to me, and my continued repentance and openness to the Holy Spirit. As I remember God's mercy, love, and forgiveness in my own life, it causes me to reach down to those who are broken and torn; so must you.

David said in Psalms 61:1—4:

"Hear my cry, O God; attend unto my prayer. From the end of the earth will I cry unto Thee, **When my heart is overwhelmed; lead me to the rock that is higher than I. For Thou has been a shelter for me, and a strong tower from the enemy.** I will abide in Thy tabernacle forever: I will trust in the covert of Thy wings. Selah."

Change Is So Wonderful, No More excess Baggage! You can Soar As An Eagle On The Wings Of God, Above The Storms, As He Brings Healing To Your Mind, Heart, Soul, and Spirit!!! Jesus is your safety net!

If you are reading this book and know you need healing for the whole person, but have not accepted Jesus as your personal Savior, ask God to come into your heart right where you are sitting and fill you with His Spirit, and He will! He has been waiting for you all the time with outstretched arms!!!!

HE IS OUR HEALER!!! YOU ARE A PERFECT CANDIDATE FOR THE HEALER... ARE YOU READY TO LET HIM BE LORD AND MASTER OF YOUR LIFE??????

HEALING PRAYER FOR THE HURTING

Father, in the Name of Jesus Christ, I praise you and I bless you for your great love for me, and the great price you paid for me at Calvary. Therefore, I come to you because you are my Abba—Father, my healer, my Savior, my friend, my redeemer, my sustainer, the eradicator of sin, my go—between, my cleanser, my peace, my hope, my perfecter, my mediator, my counselor, my High Priest, my mercy seat and my strength.

I humble myself before You, this day, making a new commitment to You. I come with a heart of thanksgiving and gratitude for all that You have been to me from my birth unto this present moment. I am presenting my whole self — heart, mind, soul, body, and spirit. I confess the lack of knowledge as how to allow Your Holy Spirit to reveal those hidden parts of me which I might not know are there and even those things that I am aware are there, in order for you to bring about the final healing and complete freedom that I so badly need in my life.

Lord, please show me what it really means to be free inwardly. I want to be free from past hurts, disappointments, fears, frustrations, jealousy, anger, bitterness, resentment, strife, unforgiveness or any other thing that would keep me from serving You with a free spirit. I am asking that You show me a new and better way. Search me and lay all things open and bare before You. You know me altogether and You know the pain I feel; therefore, I look to You as my Healer.

Lord Jesus, I want to know You in the fullness of Your power so that every part of me will be able to praise and worship You without reservations, hesitations or hindrance. There are things that have hurt me very deeply and the pain is still there, sometimes more than other times. I no longer want to confess human weakness, but I want to confess Your strength, Your power and Your forgiveness.

Lord show me those hidden things which must be dealt with by You and You alone. Search me, cleanse me and create within me a clean heart and renew within me a right spirit. I desire a heart of flesh, one that is tender and pliable. So saturate me with Your glory so that I can resist every temptation which would cause me to be impoverished in the spirit, mind, soul, and body.

Thank You Lord for Your commitment to me, for You said that if I come to You, You would not cast me out because a broken and a contrite heart You would not despise. Thank You for Your power which will enable me to walk out of any past guilt and fears, and accept Your forgiveness. Father, I know the only way I can forgive others is to appropriate Your forgiveness for my life, and forgive myself. Please heal me through and through. Thank You, Amen!!!

OTHER SCRIPTURE REFERENCES FOR READING

(King James Version)

Phillipians 3:12—14

Hebrews 4:12—16

I Samuel 1:1—17

I Samuel 16:7

Psalms 42:5—11

Psalms 51:6—17

About the Author

Delores Russ an ordained Elder for the past 32 years, currently serves as an Associate Elder at the Haven Of Rest Sanctuary Of Praise Church, Baltimore, Maryland, under the leadership of Senior Pastor Dena S. Jobes. Additional ordinations have included evangelist and pastor.

Elder Russ was founder and CEO of the Christian Women and Men In Ministry, Fellowship, Inc., an Interdenominational ministry, for 15 years, until her current duties began as a short term missionary to the continent of Africa. Elder Russ has discovered that the pain, hurt and brokenness of the thousands of African sisters are almost parallel to sisters in America, but sometimes worse because of cultural and tribal customs and traditions.

Elder Russ is much sought after for her godly wisdom, wise counsel, and her compassion and understanding for the hurting and perplexed. This handmaiden of God is known as a "spiritual mid–wife" and is fondly called "ma–ma" or mother.

Printed in the United States
33930LVS00004B/1-123

9 781420 850918